All Things Become New

AUDREY MARR

WINEPRESS WP PUBLISHING

To order additional copies of

All Things Become New

Have your credit card ready and call

1-888-242-6037

or send $10.99 each plus $3.95* S&H to

PO Box 834
St. Ignatius, MT 59865

* add $1.00 S&H for each additional book ordered

© 2000 by Audrey Marr. All rights reserved.

Printed in the United States of America.

Packaged by WinePress Publishing, PO Box 428, Enumclaw, WA 98022. The views expressed or implied in this work do not necessarily reflect those of WinePress Publishing. Ultimate design, content, and editorial accuracy of this work are the responsibilities of the author.

No part of this publication may be reproduced, stored in a retrieval system, or transmitted in any way by any means—electronic, mechanical, photocopy, recording, or otherwise—without the prior permission of the copyright holder, except as provided by USA copyright law.

Unless otherwise noted all scriptures are taken from the Holy Bible, New International Version, Copyright © 1973, 1978, 1984 by the International Bible Society. Used by permission of Zondervan Publishing House. The "NIV" and "New International Version" trademarks are registered in the United States Patent and Trademark Office by International Bible Society.

Verses marked KJV are taken from the King James Version of the Bible.

Verses marked AMP are taken from The Amplified Bible, Old Testament, Copyright © 1965 and 1987 by The Zondervan Corporation, and from The Amplified New Testament, Copyright © 1954, 1958, 1987 by The Lockman Foundation. Used by permission.

ISBN 1-57921-287-5
Library of Congress Catalog Card Number: 00-100617

*To Gary, my husband of twenty-four years and best friend.
Thank you for always believing in my potential
as a writer the seventeen years I longed to find the time
to write a book such as this.*

Hope deferred makes the heart sick,
but when the desire is fulfilled, it is a tree of life.
—Proverbs 13:12 (AMP)

Therefore if any man be in Christ,
he is a new creature:
old things are passed away;
behold, all things are become new.
—2 Corinthians 5:17 (KJV)

Acknowledgments

A special thanks to Callie Scott who made time for me at her kitchen table editing my book regardless of her large family and hectic schedule. How blessed I am to call you not only a sister-in-the-Lord but also friend. We are of kindred spirits, and I treasure what we have.

Thanks to my in-laws, Bill and Jean Marr, for their love and support. You are very dear to my heart!

A special thanks also to my unique, blessed pastor, Pete Mears of Destiny Christian Center in Ronan, Montana for his positive input—encouraging me to launch out by faith and self-publish this book.

A big thank you to my children—Mark, Rachel, David and Jesse for their great sense of humor, adjusting to a mother turned writer; always wishing me well as I went into the "ozone" at my computer.

May God receive all the glory for this book, accomplishing His good will.

... 1

THE LONE WOMAN SAT AT THE BAY WINDOW, STARING OUT AT NOTHING in particular. Her legs were drawn toward her chin, held in place with intertwined fingers, much like when she was a little girl. Her favorite pastime then was to daydream away the time in idleness by a creek near the house of her childhood. She was no longer a small child, but a woman of twenty-five years, finding herself alone. After nearly seven years of marriage, her husband and high school sweetheart, Jon Madison, had been suddenly taken from her.

Could she ever forget the day the state trooper came to her door with the news that her beloved was gone? Kara Madison was on her own. What was she to do?

A heavy sigh escaping her lips, she unfolded herself from her seat to wander around the room. The funeral had been a person's worst nightmare! Too numb to think, feel, or even speak, she was glad for the presence of family, who were now spending time with friends or relatives in the small town. Kara had opted to stay home to have some time to herself. Having been caught up in the whirlwind of events, it was now good to have some solitude, but she knew that all too soon she would have more solitude than she cared to when the family went their separate ways.

A short time later, the elder Madisons entered the house to seek out Kara in the living room. Jon's death had been a shock to everyone. All things considered, they seemed to be taking the death of their son quite well.

Alice Madison was the first to speak when she saw Kara, taking note of the dark circles under the young widow's eyes. She was filled for compassion for her dear daughter-in-law, thinking how couples so young expect to grow old together—not to endure this, the premature death of the husband, Alice's eldest son.

"I don't suppose you got any rest while we were gone or thought to eat anything, did you?"

"No, I didn't on both counts. I was trying to solve the problems of the world—mine in particular—but came to no definite conclusion or plan. My mind is spinning with everything there is to think about and the decisions I need to make." Kara was frustrated and weary.

"Give it a rest, dear. One more day isn't going to make a bit of difference."

"I have to agree with Alice. You're taking on too much, too soon. It's been a shock to us all," Jonathan Madison added. He too had a fondness for his daughter-in-law and was feeling rather helpless at the moment. Everyone was fatigued and stressed with the ordeal they had gone through only two days before.

"Come, Dear," Alice said to Kara, "let's see what's in the frig. Your co-workers were so generous to supply enough food for an army. I'm sure there's something in there that would appeal to your appetite."

. . . 2

Dave White, Kara's brother, entered the Madisons' kitchen a few hours later. At the sight of the forlorn expression on Kara's face, his first desire was to take his sister in his arms and hold her, but she seemed so distant. He knew she had built a wall of sorts to protect herself against the tears that surely wanted to flow. He had never seen a couple happier than Kara and Jon had been.

A year ago, Dave had accepted Christ as his personal Savior. He had tried to share his experience with Kara, but she stated she was quite happy the way things were and did not need this Jesus Dave wanted to talk about so much. Jonny was open to the gospel—well at least he hadn't shut Dave out when he started to witness to him.

It was only a few weeks ago he and Jon had gone on a fishing trip to a nearby lake to spend a few days. Dave had read the scripture in John 6:35: ". . . I am the bread of life. He who comes to me will never go hungry, and he who believes in me will never be thirsty." The two men had been talking about life.

Jonny was a successful businessman, with a good wife and marriage; everything seemed to come easily for him, yet he still felt a void, something lacking in his life. He was quite attentive as his brother-in-law read the scripture to him. He had wanted to hear more. As a new Christian, Dave was filled with the awe and zeal of what he read in the Bible and was more than willing to share. When all was said and done, Jon decided he wanted to do something about it. He came under conviction and desired to accept Christ as his personal Savior. Not one to waste time, Jon was ready to take action. The two young men bowed their heads before the Almighty, and with the help of his brother-in-law, Jonathan Madison, Jr. became a believer.

The last conversation Dave had had with Jon, only days before Jon's death, was a discussion about how Kara had received the news of Jon's experience with a pat-on-the-head attitude, much like his mother had done when he was young. In so many words, she expressed that it was a nice experience for him but to leave her out of it.

This grieved Dave more than the death of Jon did. He knew where his brother-in-law was for all time and eternity, but Kara was still lost.

Feeling eyes upon her, Kara turned to see a pair of compassionate blue eyes looking her way. She dearly loved this older brother of hers. Except for this religious thing Dave had gotten himself into, they were still a close-knit family. Their parents had passed away a few years ago, and now that her husband was gone, Dave was all she had. She wished he would quit looking at her with those intense blue eyes of his! It made her want to run weeping to him to hear him promise he could take the hurt away.

"You know, you really should take a break from all of this and lie down for a while. You look exhausted. Nothing is going to get done any faster when you're too tired to think."

A slight smile played on her mouth at her brother's words, which echoed the similar words of her in-laws. "I think I will, dear brother." Having said this, Kara stood and exited the room to seek her bed.

...3

AFTER HIS SISTER LEFT THE ROOM, DAVE BROUGHT UP THE SUBJECT TO those remaining at the kitchen table: Jonny's older brother, Jaime, younger brother, Jason, and, of course, Jon and Alice Madison.

"Has Kara mentioned to anyone what she's going to do now—any plans she may have made since the funeral?"

Alice was first to speak. "I don't believe she's made any plans. Personally, I think she's too tired to deal with any of it. What she could use is a vacation, some time away from here to some place where she could get rested and think clearly."

Jon, Sr. spoke next. "I think my wife is right, Dave. Alice and I thought of suggesting to Kara that she come home with us and take as much time as she needed to get her thoughts together. I'm sure she could take a leave of absence from her job, considering the circumstances."

"I can't help but wonder, though, that too much time on her hands would be worse for her. I was thinking how my auto detailing shop is getting to the point to where I'm considering hiring someone part-time to help in the office. My business partner's wife has been doing the bookwork and other necessary duties. Since Kara works at the local bank in town, I know she's more than qualified to handle the job. She's familiar with computers and assorted

. . . Audrey Marr . . .

office equipment—things I'm only beginning to learn. She could be a big help to me and hopefully teach me something along the way. I could give her some time to rest and play it by ear as to when she'd want to begin work. You know how she's always been busy, not one to be idle for long. I think it'd be good for her to have a change in scenery and a break from the painfully familiar memories around here. The mountains near my home would provide the beauty, fresh air, and exercise she's sure to need. Besides, she's talked for a long time about coming out for a visit and never made it."

After further discussion of the two options, all present agreed to approach Kara and encourage her to make a decision.

... 4

WHEN SHE SAW MONTANA, KARA WAS NOT SURE WHAT SHE HAD EXpected, but it was much more than she could have imagined. Riding in the Chevy Blazer with her brother, she was able to take in all the scenery. Bozeman was nestled in a valley of sorts with mountains all around. She had thought the mountains back east were beautiful until she saw the snow-capped Rockies. The contrast of blue sky against the white, snowy peaks was breathtaking. And the sky! It seemed so open and huge, not at all closed-in with numerous trees like in the east. She could only breathe in the crisp air from the slightly opened Blazer window and revel in the sight. It was refreshing, a healing balm upon her fatigued soul. Such a large void was ever present in the area of her heart. Would it ever go away? That old adage that time is a healer was not what she wanted to hear. What she wanted was her husband back, but that was not possible, she knew.

"So, now do you understand why I've wanted you to come out here for so long?" her brother asked, bringing her out of her revelry. "Did I lose you, Kar?"

"It's beautiful! More than I could've imagined. I mean, I've seen pictures and such, but they don't do this justice at all." It was on the tip of her tongue to say that she wished Jonny were here to see it too, but tears were always below the surface, ready to spill over at any little word or thought of him! Keeping this to herself, Kara gave her brother a smile as best she could muster.

Following a winding road nestled in the foothills heavily timbered with pine trees, they approached the enchanting house. Kara cracked the Blazer window a little wider to breathe deeply of the piney scent. "Oh Davey! This is so homey and inviting. How did you ever manage to find such a spot?"

What she saw was a log home with its stone chimney and roofed deck nestled in among the pines. Upon entering the house, she realized that looks were deceiving. It was more spacious than one might think when viewing the outside. The front door led into the living room with a wood-burning stove in the corner to the right. Various Indian-design rugs were spread on the hardwood floors with flagstone around the wood stove itself. It had something of a masculine, outdoorsy feel. Her brother, who was an avid hunter, had a number of mounts on the walls around the room. Pieces of tanned elk hide were thrown across the sofa and love seat and used as doilies under lamps and on the coffee table.

"Mmmmm, something smells good in here," Kara said as she turned to look at her brother.

"Oh, I forgot to tell you that Bobbie Brooks told me she'd have something warm in the oven waiting for us when we got here so we wouldn't have to worry about cooking. She figured we'd be too tired to take care of ourselves properly." This Dave mentioned as he picked up his sister's luggage and started in the direction of her bedroom.

Not one to waste space, Dave had made sure the log home was built with a practical layout and design. Deciding cathedral ceilings were a waste and more difficult to heat, he had a staircase built against the rear wall of the living room leading to the upstairs. At the top of the stairs was a hallway. The second story consisted of three bedrooms and two baths. It was obvious her brother had built the house with the hopes of someday having a wife and family.

The bedroom Dave chose for Kara was done in simple décor. A homemade quilt covered the full-sized bed. Along with simple muslin curtains on the two windows and a few scattered rugs on the floor, it appeared to be quite homey. In addition to the walk-in closet, drawers built into the wall were available for clothing.

"Oh, Davey! The view from here is gorgeous. I'll have to find a chair so I can sit by this window and read a book should I get the chance."

"This room looked to be one that would suit you," spoke Dave. He could not help but smile at the name only his sister had called him through the years. "It is good to have you her, Kar. I wish the circumstances were different, but I don't think you'll regret your decision to come to Montana. The fresh air does a body good. I like to take walks and hike on the trails near here when I can. Why don't you take a nap before we try Bobbie's cooking? You look all done in."

Dave had met Bobbie Brooks at a home Bible study a few months before. Sharing some of the same interests, such as hiking and other outdoor activities, they had enjoyed one another's company from time to time. The most important element was the common ground they shared in knowing the Lord as their personal Savior. It seemed the most natural thing for the two to discuss the topic of the previous Bible study and what they had gleaned from it. Her offer to have dinner waiting for them upon their arrival did wonders to warm Dave's heart. It was just like her. His sister speaking to him brought Dave to the present.

"I think I'll take you up on your suggestion and lie down for about an hour. Will that make dinner too late for you?"

"No, that's fine. You'll find out I haven't changed. I'm as laid back as ever. The bathroom is through the side door. My room is beyond it, meaning we'll share the bathroom. I've got some phone calls to make, so don't worry about me. Come downstairs whenever you like. Besides, if I get too hungry, I'll eat without you." Upon saying this, he smiled and exited, closing the door to leave Kara to herself.

The young widow heaved a heavy sigh as she kicked off her shoes and plopped on to the bed. It happened to be a feather bed, of all things. What a delight! Kara did not think she could sleep, even though she felt bone weary. She was beginning to wonder if the feeling of exhaustion would last forever.

Jonny was never far from her thoughts. Even now, she could visualize his boyish grin that was so dear to her heart. She also clearly remembered the day that the police officer came to her door to tell her of the accident. A freak mishap, they had informed her. Jonny had slipped on the wet surface of the boat and fell overboard. He was unable to free himself after he was caught under a pile of logs and drowned.

Out of habit, she reached across to feel only empty space where her husband should have been; she gave a slight shudder. Grieved too much to care if her brother could hear, she gave in to the tears and heart-wrenching sobs. Fatigue overcame the torrent of tears, and she fell into a troublesome sleep.

. . . 5

THE HOUR BECAME TWO, BUT A RESTED KARA BOUNDED DOWN THE STAIRS to seek out her brother. She found him toward the back of the house in the kitchen, which included of a number of windows in the eating area. At each window hung curtains made of dark, green calico fabric, giving the room a country appeal. An island in the center of the kitchen looked like it would be a great place to prepare meals. The kitchen cabinets were in an L-shape. A forest green kitchen counter and almond-colored appliances added to the homey appearance.

Dave was seated at the oak table with a young woman, whom Kara assumed to be Bobbie. Her guess was confirmed when Dave stood upon seeing her enter the kitchen, his obvious concern apparent as he studied her face. Seemingly satisfied at what he saw, he smiled in relief as he spoke.

"Kar, or maybe I should say, Kara, this is Bobbie Brooks, a friend of mine. We met at the Wednesday night Bible study I attend in Belgrade. Bobbie, this is my sister I've told you about. I've already mentioned she's going to stay for a few months to rest up and help at the shop."

Kara was immediately taken with the woman who stood before her. Bobbie had long blonde hair pulled back in a French braid,

deep blue eyes that sparkled, and a slim, tall frame that wore casual blue jeans and sweatshirt.
"Hi, Kara. I'm pleased to meet you. Dave has told me so much about you, and don't worry—all of it was good," Bobbie informed her with a warm, genuine smile as she extended her hand to greet her. "And I hope you like casseroles since I forgot to ask Dave about it. Actually, it's chicken pot pie along with a salad and applesauce." This said, she brought the casserole from the oven to the table.
Dave gave his sister a sheepish grin and proceeded to explain, "I was too hungry to wait for you. After about an hour, I checked on you to be sure you were OK. You looked as though you were out like a light, so I let you sleep, and I ate without you."
"That's quite all right, brother," Kara said, as she gave him a quick hug before taking a seat at the kitchen table. "You said you'd eat without me if you got too hungry, so no apologies are necessary. I know right now I'm starved myself. This food smells delicious, Bobbie."
The three chatted amiably over cups of coffee while Kara ate, enjoying the time together. Clean up went quickly, and the trio exited to the living room to various pieces of furniture. There were a love seat and sofa of Southwest design and four chairs handmade of wooden branches with a similar design on the cushions. The wood stove burning cheerily made the room cozy and familiar, as the days were still cool, especially the evenings.
The weekend ahead of them, the three thought it would be a good idea to take advantage of the time off and do some sightseeing and hiking. Kara had always been active, enjoying most outdoor activities. It was nearly 11 P.M. when Bobbie took leave and the two siblings retired for the night.

... 6

Saturday dawned sunny and pleasant, although the April air still had a bite to it. After a breakfast of fresh fruit and bagels, Dave helped Kara pack lunches, and they were soon on their way.

Bobbie had agreed to meet them at the foot of a hiking trail both she and Dave were familiar with. She was waiting for them upon their arrival. Kara was glad she had packed warm clothes for her trip west on this brisk morning, for she was able to see her breath.

"Good morning, Bobbie," Dave said cheerily.

Kara was only a step behind her brother and was eager to get started. After a quick hello to their companion, they wasted no time and began the hike.

Given a little time, Kara believed she and Bobbie could be good friends. The woman seemed so warm and caring. Kara felt comfortable with her.

Bobbie had taken the lead, with Kara in the middle and Dave bringing up the rear. As they hiked the trail Bobbie carried on light conversation with Kara, describing the different types of pine trees in the area, as well as the birds. It was an enjoyable time. After the space of an hour or so, the trio opted to take a short break, relaxing on an outcropping of rock alongside the trail, basking in the sunshine.

Kara was enjoying herself and it showed in the broad smile, her cheeks rosy from the cool air and exertion.

"You look rather content sitting there," Dave commented, grinning at his sister.

"I am," Kara said blissfully. "This is a cool place to cross-country ski in the winter when the snow is too deep to walk. As we go further up the trail, you'll see the various paths going off in different directions," Dave informed his sister.

"Really?" Bobbie asked. "That's something I've never tried before. I've done plenty of downhill skiing at the local ski resort. Come to think of it, Dennis Cooper and a couple others at Bible study mentioned they like to cross-country ski."

At the mention of the Bible study, before the two got deeply engrossed in the subject Kara had no desire to discuss, she jumped to a standing position and suggested they walk some more.

Kara took the lead this time. Bobbie and Dave seemed to chat like old friends, and one could see they enjoyed the companionship. After another thirty minutes, they decided to break for lunch. Dave had a backpack full of goodies, since he had agreed to pack most of the food. He had not gotten any argument from the women. They stopped by a small creek that flowed quietly along in no definite pattern, disappearing in time under a rock covering. The air seemed fresh and heavy with a piney scent. Kara wondered if she would ever get enough of the smell of these woods that were so different from the ones back east.

After a light lunch of ham sandwiches and yogurt, the trio decided to go back in the direction of the vehicles. "I'll take the lead this time, ladies," spoke Dave firmly. "With all the food the two of you ate, I should be able to stay way out in front."

"Oh, aren't we a smart one today? I don't think you have walked far enough yet if you still have energy to criticize our eating habits," remarked Kara as she gave her brother a light punch on the arm.

Everyone laughed.

When the three got to the end of the trail, Bobbie extended an invitation to her place for dinner. She promised it would be a simple fare, but filling and nutritious. Dave and Kara decided to take Bobbie up on the offer. Once arriving at the apartment, Dave was elected to cook the burgers on the grill kept on the back deck while the women enjoyed chatting as they fixed baked potatoes and green beans.

A full stomach went a long way to providing contentment. Kara found herself suddenly exhausted and ready to retire. Both Bobbie and Dave noticed her fatigue, so the visit was cut short as Dave hastened to usher Kara home to bed.

Too weary to take a shower, Kara found that a feather bed had never felt so wonderful. Kara was sure that with a good night's rest she would feel better in the morning, possibly not quite so exhausted. She felt as though she had made the right choice in coming to Montana and was content with the realization. Life goes on, and she would try to make the best of it. This was Kara's last thought as she drifted off to sleep, her arm stretched across the vacancy beside her.

... 7

THE SUN WAS SHINING BRIGHT AND CHEERY THROUGH THE BEDROOM WINdow when Kara awoke the next morning. For just a moment, in her drowsiness, she forgot where she was and why she was there. The memory of it all suddenly flooded her mind, and she wished she could forget all of it, pretend it had never happened. But that was not reality and wishing was not going to change the fact that she was indeed a widow. All she felt this morning was emptiness, a dull ache about the spot where her heart was. What she wanted to do was roll over in the bed and cry until she couldn't cry anymore, but the more practical side of her took over for the moment and she leaped out of bed. Maybe it was because she had gotten a good night's sleep, but then . . . who knows. She was never one to be idle for long and had been actively involved in a number of community activities back home.

Following a long, warm shower, Kara donned jeans and sweatshirt and hustled downstairs. With the house so quiet, she suddenly remembered the conversation she and her brother had had on the way home from Bobbie's apartment the night before. Dave had gently reminded her that the next day was Sunday, a day when he liked to go to church and not sleep in. He mentioned that she was more than welcome to come along, but she had quickly made excuses why she couldn't. It appeared as though she had the house all to herself this morning. Her brother had said he would not be home until close to one o'clock and she should make herself at home. After searching the refrigerator for something to eat, Kara sat down to a breakfast of a bagel and juice. She noticed a note alongside the Sunday paper:

> Kar, hope you had a good night's sleep. Be sure to enjoy the morning with a short walk or something. Maybe you need some time alone anyway. I'll be home as soon as I can. Davey

A walk did sound pleasant to her. There was a part of her that seemed foreign though, a part that desired to be lazy and vegetate. She thought a warm shower would have refreshed her, but the fatigue still lingered. Oh, well. She had best get on with her day. After breakfast she would take that walk and then surprise her brother by seeing what she could cook up for lunch.

✣   ✣   ✣

Feeling invigorated after a brisk walk, Kara set about to prepare soup and sandwiches for lunch.

Dave entered the house calling his sister's name. He was surprised to find her standing over a pan on the stove, stirring something.

"This is a pleasant surprise. I was hoping you'd take it easy and allow me to get lunch, or were you too hungry and impatient to wait?" he teased as he approached her, resting his arm across her shoulders.

"Uh-huh. It's real hard to open a can of soup and stir it on the stove, brother."

"Sometimes, I wonder if you know what the words *take it easy* mean though. You still look a bit tired to me." Following this comment, he bent over to smell the soup, savoring the delicious aroma.

"Why don't you set the table so we can eat? I've got the sandwiches put together too, so everything is ready."

Dave mentioned that she should not hesitate to browse through the kitchen cupboards and find what she needed. In a few minutes, they were sitting down to eat the roast beef and cheese sandwiches Kara had prepared. Then Dave asked if his sister minded if he gave thanks for the food. It was his house, of course, so Kara graciously consented. It seemed odd to hear her brother talking to God like He was a real person in the flesh. *You'd think God Himself was present at the table*, she thought. Well, at least the prayer was short and to the point. It seemed to her the food set before them was put there by hard work, not the hand of God. She kept these thoughts to herself though as the "Amen" was said and they began to eat. They had mostly small talk during the meal.

Dave did suggest that since it was such a nice day, they should go for a Sunday afternoon drive. It would allow Kara to take in some of the city of Bozeman as well as the surrounding area. There were quaint shops downtown to browse in and the ever-famous discount stores too. Kara thought it was a great idea, so after the kitchen was tidied, they were on their way.

❖ ❖ ❖

Kara had forgotten how much fun it was to be around her brother. Since he had moved to Montana four years ago, they had only had phone conversations until this year. It was good to laugh and chat with him in person. They were only eighteen months apart in age. Dave was tall enough to be called "big." He stood six feet two inches in his stocking feet. Having always been athletic, he looked the part with his broad shoulders. She was sure he had broken many a girl's heart through the years with his good looks: brown hair with blonde highlights much like hers and an easy smile displaying white, even teeth. Kara herself was of average height, though she appeared taller because of her long, slender legs.

The brother and sister were able to browse in a number of small but fascinating shops along Main Street and then proceeded to their favorite discount store. Kara had a few personal items to buy and then suggested they go somewhere to eat—her treat. Not one to ever turn down such an offer, Dave opted for a Chinese restaurant in town. The food was delicious and each other's company enjoyable, so they took their time eating.

"Oh, Davey, this is wonderful. I'm so glad you chose this place."

Dave smiled, love for his sister apparent. "I'm glad you like it. I assume you also like this fair city?"

"Yes," spoke Kara, her eyes sparkling with delight. "I'm sure the history of the place is interesting. Maybe we could go to the mall sometime soon. I'd like that."

"Sure. I'd be glad to take you."

A sudden thought occurred to Kara and she giggled.

"What's so funny, Kar? Come on and clue me in."

"Nothing really. Out of the blue, I just remembered how at one time I was bigger and taller than you were. Do you remember the scrap we got into and I shoved you so hard you fell backward into an empty box? I can still see the look of horror on your face to find yourself weaker than I."

"Yeah. I also remember, correct me if I'm wrong, the many times you took advantage of the boxing gloves I got for Christmas one year and beat me to a pulp. I lost count as to how often that happened. I imagine you relished the moment every time you pounded me."

"Yes," Kara commented, her eyes twinkling, "and I knew it was wise to quit picking on you when you got stronger and taller."

Dave put his head back and laughed at his sister's honesty. Glancing at his watch, Dave thought they should take their leave. After a quick stop at he grocery store, the two went in the direction of home.

Kara was taking a ready liking to Dave's house and surroundings and told him as much after settling on the sofa in the comfortable living room, along with a cup of herbal tea, shortly after they arrived home. Following the death of their parents, Dave had used his share of the inheritance to purchase the land and log home package. He was able to do a lot of the work himself with the help from friends, when they were available. He had never had a problem getting to know people and making friends anyway.

"You know, Kar, the Lord has been good to me. I thank Him all the time for what I have. I wasn't a believer when I got established here in Montana, but looking back, I can see the Lord was with me.

I got a real deal on the property and everything kind of fell into place for me. My business has done very well for me too. I've found that what Dad used to say is true—that if you treat people fairly, honestly and with integrity, you'll go a long way."

Kara smiled at the mention of their father. "I sure do miss Daddy. He always made me feel I was special and loved. Mom did too, of course, but I guess there's something different between a father and daughter."

Nodding his head in agreement, Dave spoke. "It's hard to believe it's been five years since they passed away. I miss them too."

"By the way, I've got to get back to work tomorrow and make sure Drew is staying in line and treating our customers right. I want you to get rested up, and we'll take things a day to a time. There's no sense rushing into things. Sandy isn't going to take a leave of absence for another couple of weeks, which gives you plenty of time. I have a woman who comes in once a week to clean house and tidy this place too, so there isn't all that much that's required of you. Kind of like a lady of leisure."

Dave wore an impish grin following the last comment.

"Davey, I can't become a wallflower. I never was one and I'm not about to begin now. I'll appease you and take a few days more, and then I expect to go with you to the job. I'm certain I can save you a few dollars by keeping house myself. I don't mind doing it and it will save you some money. I'll be sure to have your dinner waiting for you when you get home, which is about what time?"

"Six o'clock."

"Good. That'll give me plenty of time to get organized. I feel like I'm still suffering from jet lag, or something."

"It's probably the time change—you know, there is a difference of two hours."

Once the conversation lagged, Kara's eyes drooped a bit, and the two decided to get themselves to bed. Kara snuggled under the quilt, feeling quite content. It crossed her mind how much she missed having a solid warmth next to her, but she was too tired to deal with it and quickly fell into a deep slumber.

... 8

K ARA HAD ALWAYS BEEN A SOUND SLEEPER. IT DIDN'T SURPRISE HER THAT her brother had left for work and it was nearly 9 A.M. when she opened her eyes.

"Golly, Kar, you had better get a grip on yourself or your brother is going to have to drag you out of bed to get you to work on time. You'll be making him late."

Maybe it was because of the recent events. Kara had never been late for work once in the seven years she had worked at the First National Bank back home, but she still felt better giving herself a scolding. She had already made a mental list of various duties she wanted to accomplish today, like laundry and tidying the house a bit.

As she went about her chores, the young widow thought about some of the special times in her life with her late husband. It was an odd feeling to think of oneself as a widow. She had eyes only for Jonny, even while dating for two years in high school. It seemed so special right from the start. He was the new kid in town, yet he seemed confident and sure of himself. Their first meeting was face to face after she had gotten a drink from the school water fountain in the hallway. In her rush, she turned suddenly to bump into the chest of the person she had not known was there. Embarrassed, she looked up to apologize and gaze into the blue eyes of a stranger. This flustered her more than ever as she stammered an apology and left in a hurry, thinking as she did so that he must be the new student all the girls were chattering about. He probably thought she had bumped into him on purpose too!

At the end of the school day, she heard an unfamiliar voice behind her as she was putting her books into her locker.

"Hi. Since you didn't give me time to speak to you earlier, I thought I'd let you know that your apology was accepted. Do you always rush everywhere you're going?"

"Well, no. In fact, I was afraid you'd think I'd done it on purpose." Kara had always liked blue eyes. Hers were a green color. She noted the raven black hair that had a bit of curl to it. She was brought out of her thoughts when the young man questioned her.

"I'm sorry. I don't know your name. My name is Jonathan Madison, but Jon is what most people call me. And your name is?"

"Oh, I'm Kara White. Nice to meet you. Welcome to the community."

"Thanks. You wouldn't mind showing me some of the sights in town, would you? I understand this is a tourist town and there's plenty to see."

Kara thought at first he must be joking and trying to make a move on her, yet he looked too sincere, almost innocent. "No, I wouldn't mind at all. Uh, sometime, that is."

The sometime was that very weekend. Kara was able to use the family car to drive Jon around to see the sights. He was great company and entertaining with all the stories of the mischief he'd done, mostly childhood antics. It appeared that Jon Madison was a real character and knew how to make people laugh.

It was not long before the two had an understanding and everyone else was aware of it as well. They were often seen together with one family or the other. It became acceptable in the parents' eyes that the two would someday join in matrimony. Graduation was in May, and they were married in September of the same year. Kara had successfully acquired a job at the local bank, and Jonny, as she liked to call him, found employment at one of the car dealers in town. He seemed to have a natural charisma with people and selling cars. It came as easily as tying one's shoes for him.

... All Things Become New ...

Now here she was twenty-four hundred miles from home, and she had no husband. She had yet to come to a conclusion about her future. Her boss had assured her the job would be waiting for her when she got back, so that did not present a problem. At the moment, she could not imagine being married to anyone else. She and Jonny had talked about it now and then, but they had had every intention of growing old together. Well, let tomorrow take care of itself. She still had a number of small jobs to do about the house, so she'd best keep at it.

Kara had a sandwich for lunch while she browsed through the local paper. Afterward, she put a beef roast in the oven for dinner. It was Davey's favorite, along with all the extras like mashed potatoes, green beans with crisped bacon, and coleslaw. She could do with a bread machine too but decided they would have to survive without fresh bread. She was already feeling weary and it would be several hours before her brother would get home.

The two large picture windows in the living room allowed plenty of sunshine and light to enter the room. Kara decided to relax on the sofa for a half-hour or so. She promised herself that was all the time she needed, and then she'd get back to her "to do" list.

A while later, Kara woke with a start. Looking at the clock on the wall, she saw it was after 3 P.M. Why, she'd nearly slept the afternoon away! And there were still things that needed to be done. Ashamed of herself and wondering at her laziness, Kara set to work. By the time Dave entered the house promptly at 6 P.M., dinner was ready to put on the table.

"Wow! It sure is nice to come home to a hot meal. You're going to spoil me for sure. I'm used to hamburgers or frozen dinners on weekdays."

Kara laughed, looking rather smug. "Did you think I had forgotten how to cook in the past few weeks? What you really need is a wife to come home to, someone to spoil you better than I ever could."

Davey frowned a little at the statement. It was not that he did not want to marry. He had not found a person with whom he wanted to spend the rest of his life. Since becoming a Christian, he had petitioned the Lord often about his desire for a wife. Feeling certain the Lord had someone for him, he was more than willing to wait rather than make a mistake and regret his choice. It was then the face of Bobbie Brooks came to mind. One never knew . . .

Like old times when they were growing up, the brother and sister shared conversation during the meal. Davey told Kara about the events of the day at work and the business in general. It seemed his business partner had not missed him much in his absence, or so he said, but it looked like there was plenty of work to do. It was good to be busy anyway.

Kara offered to deal with the dishes and tidy the kitchen while her brother took a shower.

It was another relaxing evening together. In no time, Davey had a fire going in the wood stove. He had propane heat, but something about the wood heat made the room so cozy. The evening passed quickly as the two watched a video and sipped on mugs of hot tea.

After the two-hour nap she had had, Kara didn't think she would be able to sleep, but following a warm shower, it seemed the best choice. The feather bed was always comfortable. She went to sleep with her arm where Jonny should have been, thinking she would have to get a feather mattress for herself when she returned home again, wherever home was.

. . . 9

On Wednesday, Kara decided to go through her mail, which had been sent to Montana via a girlfriend back home. From what she could gather, she would not have to worry about her financial state. The life insurance policy Jonny had from his job provided a sizeable sum of money. She wondered if she should invest the policy money and make do with her paycheck when she started working for Davey. It surely would not take too much for her to live. There were matters she had never considered when Jonny died, things her father-in-law saw to since she was not of the presence of mind to think straight.

Kara had no doubts or misgivings about having come west with Davey. He had always been supportive of her, had always encouraged her in little ways, had understood her as only a brother could. Thinking about it, she was ready to begin learning the booking system and running of Davey's business. She'd tell him this evening. Jonny was still a painful memory, accompanied by a small measure of guilt. It was all too much to want to sit and analyze now. It was too soon—much too soon.

The telephone interrupted her thoughts. Her in-laws were faithfully calling, sometimes every day, to check up on her, wanting to know how everything was going, expressing their love, and reminding her that she was more than welcome to visit them for a spell too. It was nice to be wanted.

✢   ✢   ✢

Davey was surprised when his sister suggested she come to work with him the next day. He felt it was too soon. Kara still looked tired to him. Oh, sure, he knew she was an active person, but he felt obligated as her brother to take special care of her and even pamper her a bit if he could. She, however, had other ideas. He reluctantly agreed to allow her to begin the next day. At least there were only two workdays remaining, though he sometimes worked half a day on Saturdays. He had thanked the Lord many times for his Christian business partner who was sensitive to the circumstances involving his sister.

The day was busy, causing Davey to look forward to the fellowship and relaxation of spending time in the Bible with his Christian friends.

After a stop at home for a meatloaf dinner Kara had prepared and a quick shower, Davey left for the 7:30 P.M. Bible study feeling a bit guilty about leaving his sister alone for the evening. Kara had assured him that she would be fine and that he needed his own life. She encouraged him to live as he had before she came to be with him.

Fatigue seemed to always be with her these days. After the kitchen was once again neat and tidy, she looked about for something to read. There were several shelves of books in the living room. Choosing one of several classics she found, Kara sat down to enjoy reading after turning the volume on the stereo low. It wasn't long before her eyes were drooping though. Not bothering to wait up for her brother, she went off to bed before 9 P.M., always aware of the empty space beside her and the void in her life.

✢   ✢   ✢

Davey enjoyed Wednesday night Bible study. First they worshipped accompanied by a guitar and then they studied the Word. It amazed him how little he knew. There seemed to be a lot to learn, and reading the Bible was never boring for him. It seemed full of hidden treasures for the reader and difficult to get enough of it.

His sister was never far from his thoughts since the death of Jon. He felt so burdened for her, as well as protective. She was very vulnerable and needed the Lord as her personal Savior, though she could not see that right now. Davey found himself praying constantly for her.

Among those who attended the Bible study, there was a common bond of love for the Lord, so he felt comfortable sharing what was on his heart. The response he got from the others was a bit overwhelming. Dennis Cooper, a layman in the church Davey attended, led the Bible study. He had an open, honest face and was the kind of person who would look you in the eye when speaking to you. You could see the love of God reflected in his eyes. He voiced his support for Davey and made it clear that they all had been praying not only for Kara but also for Davey, and would continue to do so. Following the meeting, they all enjoyed finger foods and the fellowship of one another. Bobbie Brooks approached Davey.

"Dave, I wanted you to know how much I like your sister. I had a good time with the two of you the other day. She is just the way you described her to me and seems so sweet."

Davey's face lit up with pleasure. "Thanks, Bobbie. We had a great time too. It was good for Kara to get out for some exercise. I had told her a little about you before you met."

"So . . . how are *you* doing, Dave, with the loss of your brother-in-law? It's not just your sister who is hurting, I'm sure. People tend to forget a death affects not only the immediate family but extended family as well."

"Yeah, I guess you're right about that. I hadn't given it much thought with my concern for Kara's emotional state." Suddenly feeling weary, Davey rubbed the back of his neck. "Jon was a great guy. I couldn't have asked for a better brother-in-law. He and Kara were close. It was kind of neat to watch the two of them together. Jon could take a joke and could dish it out too. We had some good times. I have thanked the Lord many times over since his death, knowing that some day I will see him again. After all, he is where we as Christians want to be—with the Lord!"

"I guess one has to remember the good times and dwell on them."

Davey nodded his head in agreement.

"On a lighter note, Dave, how about the three of us getting together Saturday night for dinner and—if you and Kara are up to it—bowling."

"Sure. That sounds like fun."

The thought did enter his mind that it would be great to spend time alone with Bobbie—just the two of them. He had so little time with her before the death of Jon. With a sigh, he decided it was something that would have to wait. Kara needed him.

❖   ❖   ❖

Having set the alarm the night before, Kara had made it a priority to be up in plenty of time so as not to slow down her brother. She prepared a quick breakfast and set about to put food in the slow cooker for dinner.

Dave was up and ready to go by the time Kara completed her preparations. Work was only a twenty-minute drive. T&W Auto Creations shop was simple enough on the outside. The size of the building looked to be more than sufficient for the needs. Entering through a door with an office sign above it on the outside, Kara approached the counter. She had never had trouble making friends or meeting new people. After all, it had been part of her job for years as a bank teller.

Dave spoke first to the woman at the desk beyond the counter. "Hi, Sandy. Looks like you've got company today in the form of my sister here. Kara, this is Sandy Toomey. Sandy, this is Kara Madison, you know, the one I was telling you about for a few years—now in person."

A very pregnant Sandy stood to greet Kara. She too was of average height, with black hair and dark, liquid brown eyes set in the longest, most attractive eyelashes Kara had ever seen on a woman. Her smile was infectious; one could not help but smile in return. Kara felt bad that the woman had made the effort to rise in her behalf. Davey had mentioned she was due to have the baby in another two months, but Kara would not have believed it. She was secretly glad she had decided to start today and not put it off any longer, believing she had done the right thing for Sandy's sake, if for no other reason. Sandy was the wife of Davey's business partner. Sandy and her husband had yet to decide whether or not Sandy would return to the office after the baby was born.

"Kara, I'm so glad we finally meet! Dave has spoken about you often and I have wished I could meet you. I'm sorry for the way things have gone for you."

Somehow, Kara believed the woman. She had heard so many sympathies, she thought she could scream, but hearing Sandy's words spoken in kindness and sincerity made her feel special—as if Sandy meant every word.

Dave suggested Kara speak to his buddy, Drew, before she began work in the office. He escorted her to the shop area where his business partner was already at work. Kara remembered Drew from back home. Drew and Davey had attended high school together. Both had a liking for auto bodywork and were often seen together under or around a car. It was not uncommon to have Drew join their family for dinner since the Whites' garage had two bays, one of which was always occupied by a car the guys had found somewhere to work on. Following high school, the two found employment at a local auto body shop to gain experience and specialized training as well as to learn the angles of the business.

They chose auto detailing over all. Both had a knack for the job. When they were about twenty-two years old, after saving every spare dime, they felt they had enough to start their own business. A friend in Montana had invited them to come for a visit and see if they would like to set up shop in that state. Being young and adventuresome had its advantages. They liked the people and the state itself so much they decided Montana was for them. Each man complemented the other, making it a workable and now a profitable business.

When Drew met his future wife, Sandy, he became aware of his need for the Lord. The young woman did much to help him realize that being moral, good, and fair was not enough. She lived her walk; one couldn't help but love her. It was the love of God shining through her that was the major attraction, although Sandy herself was always a fun person to be with. Through an invitation to a Bible study, Drew suddenly had a spiritual hunger that would not be quenched until he accepted the Lord into his heart and life. From then it was only a matter of time until he was seriously pursuing Sandy. Within a year they were married.

"Still messing with cars and paint I see," Kara stated with a smile as she came upon the man painting a pickup truck.

Drew gave her a broad grin as he removed his respirator. "Well, Kar, good to see you! Do you remember seeing me any other way?" Suddenly serious, he asked in sincere concern, "How are you doing, Kar?" as he wrapped her in a bear hug.

Dear Drew. He was always like having another brother around. She could not remember how many times he had teased her while growing up. Before Jonny came along, some folks, including her parents, had thought the two would someday be more than friends, but Kara had had the distinct feeling that nothing was a match for Drew's attention like a car with a 454 engine, racing stripes, and wide tires. She supposed there was a time when she had had a mild crush on him, but then again, he was just brotherly Drew, the kid that was always around. Most of the time, only his feet were visible, as he worked on his cars.

Kara tried to put Drew at ease upon releasing her. "I'm doing OK. I can't say it's always easy, but being with Davey again has been wonderful."

Drew seemed satisfied with her answer and grinned before speaking. "Yeah, Dave will do."

After making small talk of news back home, Kara decided she should get back to the office. After all, that's why she was there. The shop area, like the office, was surprisingly neat. Davey had always had a thing about being tidy. Sandy set to work between telephone interruptions to show Kara the bookkeeping system on the computer. Before the two realized it, it was noon and time for a break. Davey suggested they order pizza.

After they received the pizza delivery, the four sat on whatever was handy around the office to enjoy the camaraderie, laughing and joking. Kara felt as though she had known Sandy all her life. Drew had certainly done well for himself. The coming first baby was an exciting topic. The subject of choosing names entered the conversation, as did an invitation to dinner when it was convenient. Kara mentioned it should be something easy and informal.

... All Things Become New ...

Sandy worked until 2 P.M. After that, the guys answered the telephone and took care of customers. She suggested she and Kara do a little shopping until Dave was finished with work. Kara, who was beginning to lag again, agreed the shopping would perk her up. Would she ever feel rested again?

Like schoolgirls off on a shopping spree, the two women did a lot of browsing, especially in the infant departments of several stores. It had been a while since Kara had had so much fun. She felt very comfortable around Sandy. After some conversation, she realized that she and Sandy were the same age. She was able to get caught up in the excitement of the baby-on-the-way. The time flew by and before either one realized it, it was time to get back to the shop. Sandy left Kara at the office, while she herself went home to get dinner started. The men cleaned up the shop for the day just before closing time.

Kara felt a sort of contentment, like she had accomplished something important today. Maybe she had crossed an invisible hurdle today. She was tired, but happy.

Dinner was tasty and enjoyable. Then the brother and sister shared the chore of clean up. They exited to the living room to watch a video about places to see in Montana. The ghost towns sounded like fun places to visit. And one could still pan for gold, just like the early pioneer days. About 9 P.M., Kara was glad to call it a day, always extending her arm to the empty space beside her.

✜   ✜   ✜

Friday flew by, with Sandy and Kara working well together in the office.

Davey and Kara had another quiet evening at home. Davey suggested she sleep in on Saturday morning. He had a deadline to meet on one of the jobs at the shop, so he would work until noon. He reminded her that Bobbie had invited them for dinner. They had already decided that Italian food would be great. Kara had agreed to fix a salad for the meal.

Kara had no problem sleeping in the next day. It was nearly 9:30 A.M. before she stirred. Rolling over to see the clock on the bedside stand, she was suddenly wide awake when she saw the time.

There was laundry to catch up on and phone calls to make; the house could use some cleaning too. Davey was home before she realized that for the second time that day, time had gotten away from her.

Bobbie made lasagna for the meal. Along with the French bread and salad, it made for a sumptuous meal. After clean up and another cup of coffee, the three decided bowling would be fun, especially after eating so much.

Kara had a fair ability when it came to bowling. She proved to be more than a match for her brother and Bobbie. Following a series of Kara's strikes in the second game, Davey asked in surprise, "Wow, Kar! When did you become such a pro at bowling?"

"The past couple of years I was on a women's bowling team, or had you forgotten? I never got as good as some of my teammates, but I can hold my own."

"That's not fair, Kara," spoke Bobbie with a fake pout on her face. "Dave never told me I would be up against a pro."

The three broke out in laughter. It proved to be a fun evening for everyone. Following three games, Davey suggested they have dessert at a local restaurant. Kara threatened she was going to gain weight in no time if everyone kept feeding her the way they were. But the hot fudge brownie treat was delicious! She made certain Bobbie was seated next to her brother. The thought crossed her mind that maybe she should allow the two some space and time alone. She would be discrete about it but was sure it could happen. Bobbie was so likeable.

Later, the thought of being a matchmaker appealed to Kara as she settled under the covers for the night. It also created an emptiness and pang around the area of her heart. *Maybe with time it gets better,* she told herself for the hundredth time since becoming a widow.

... 10

AFTER A BUSY WEEKEND, KARA WAS READY TO TACKLE THE BOOKWORK at the auto body shop. As the days passed, the brother and sister took on a routine. Since they had always enjoyed being together growing up, it was not hard for the two to get along and assume the necessary roles. Kara felt good about saving her brother money by cleaning the house and doing the laundry. She was compensated for her time spent at the office, which made her feel independent as well. She was beginning to think she could like Montana.

Her in-laws questioned her now and then about her future plans, but for the time being she had none. The idea of going back to her house in the east was a painful thought, as well as a comforting one. To be around the familiar would be good, but the idea of Jonny not being there to greet her was almost unbearable. Davey had assured her that she could take all the time she needed to decide. There was no hurry as far as he was concerned. Not feeling pressured to make a hasty decision was a comfort. It would overwhelm her so at times; she felt like she was being rolled over with wave after wave of different emotions. She appreciated her brother's concern and love, but realized she needed to have a discussion with him—soon.

✣   ✣   ✣

The opportunity arose a few days later when Kara sought her brother in his office at home. It was a small room off the kitchen, allowing him a certain amount of privacy, as well as enabling him to accomplish some business at home. She was sure that a lot of his time was spent in conversation with a certain blonde.

Davey motioned her to take a seat as he finished his telephone conversation. Hanging up the phone, Davey turned his attention to his sister. "So, what brings you in here? The last I noticed, you had your nose in a book, deeply engrossed. Before you answer my question though, I wanted to ask you lest I forget. Would you be interested in going on a hayride next Saturday? Anyone is welcome to come. We're having a wiener roast following the hayride. Bobbie, Sandy, and Drew will be there. What do you think?"

Well, it did sound like fun and something out of the ordinary. Kara could not remember the last time she had been on a hayride. "Sure, it sounds like fun so long as it doesn't get too religious, you know?"

"I don't know what you mean by religious," Dave said with a shrug of his shoulders. "We'll sing some simple songs and read a portion of Scripture from the Bible, but I don't think you'll find it offensive. What I mean is, have Sandy, Drew, or Bobbie ever been offensive to you?"

"No, I can't say they have. Actually, they have been a lot of fun to be with. I'd probably be a miserable mess if you hadn't a social life and friends like you do out here."

Davey appreciated this comment.

"But this all brings me to the reason why I've torn myself away from my fiction book to be sitting here." Davey's interest was piqued now. "I dearly love you brother, but for however long I'm going to stay here with you, I feel you need to have some sort of life of your own. Both you and Bobbie are always willing to have a tagalong and never make me feel like 'three's a crowd', but you do need some space. I could use some quiet time. There's always the television or a good book. I think I need to adjust to being alone again and I promise I won't live with you forever!"

"It's just like you, Kar, to always rush things. Seven weeks isn't a long time after spending nearly seven years with Jon. My social life isn't suffering as much as you would like to believe. But I do appreciate your honesty. If I ever have a problem with the way things are, I'll let you know. I love you, Kar, and want to help you as much as I can. Besides, it's not like I'm such an old man that I feel like life is passing me by. Don't let things bother you so much, OK?"

Kara nodded her head. Had anyone ever had such a special brother as she? Feeling it was a good time to exit before she started crying, something she had not allowed herself the privilege of doing in a while, Kara settled on the sofa with a book in hand, although the thought of reading was far from her mind. She soon gave it up as a lost cause and went to bed. Then she allowed the tears to flow as she reached across the empty bed, hugging a pillow to herself to quiet her sobs. It was some time before she drifted off to sleep.

... 11

THE WEEK FLEW BY AND BEFORE THE BROTHER AND SISTER KNEW IT, IT was Saturday. In the early afternoon, the pair decided to plant a small garden. Even in May the tender plants could freeze, so care would have to be taken to protect them by covering the plants in the evenings before the temperature got too cold. Into the ground they planted the beans, squash, carrots, and pea seeds. The earthy smell of the dirt and the feel of it through her fingers were pleasant to Kara. She had always enjoyed working in her mother's flowers while growing up, eventually preparing her own flowerbed after she married. Eventually, these flowers and green plants thrived under her care, and she felt an accomplishment, a satisfaction, watching the seedlings grow.

On this day, Dave showed his sister how to make a small hole in the dirt for each garden plant. They crouched in the dirt, working as a team, to cover the fragile roots of the tender plants with dirt, feeling a sense of self-satisfaction. Finishing the job, Davey put the garden tools away in the shed while Kara fixed sandwiches for lunch.

After snacking on turkey sandwiches, the two lounged around the house until time to get ready for the hayride. Kara secretly wished she could have taken the liberty to nap, but felt she had already been sleeping enough for a lifetime lately.

... All Things Become New ...

Evenings were still cool. Kara pulled her light brown hair back in a ponytail and donned a sweatshirt, jeans, and hiking shoes. She was excited and ready to go as she hastened to join her brother. Snatching her coat from the closet, she left the house with Dave and a bag of snack foods.

The ranch was about a forty-five-minute drive. The place was situated against the foothills of a mountain range. The main part of the ranch was on the flats, with gently rolling hills that led into the mountains. Dave had not been to the place for a while and was excited to show his sister. The owner attended Dave's church and Wednesday night Bible study. Along with his parents and a ranch hand, they operated the two-thousand-acre ranch, raising cattle and some horses. Extra hay was put up to sell during the winter months.

Kara thought the place had a western, nostalgic look to it. She could see the main house, a modular home, and several outbuildings, as well as corrals. Everything seemed to be well ordered and kept up. It all had a homey appeal too.

Several people had already arrived. Kara was a bit hesitant to get out of the Blazer, suddenly feeling shy. She was relieved to see an excited Sandy waving at her, motioning for her to join she and Drew as they stood chatting with another couple.

Upon approaching Sandy, Kara thought she would have never believed someone could get so big with a pregnancy. "Sandy, I can't believe you're still walking around! It seems you are either brave or a little foolish to be here."

Sandy laughed good-naturedly. "Hi, Kara, it's good to see you too. Actually, home isn't all that far away should I go into labor, and I'm sure I'll have plenty of time. Besides, I've been given an estimated due date—three more weeks or so, although I have to admit I've been ready for a number of weeks to get this little one out in the open and into my arms."

The two women had been in some interesting discussions over the weeks about Sandy and Drew's plan to have a home birth with an experienced midwife. They had done a lot of research and had worked with the midwife throughout the pregnancy. Sandy had told her that home birthing was gaining popularity in the area. To give birth in familiar surroundings was a convenient and comfortable option for some. Kara found the topic quite interesting. She could not help feeling some envy. For the past few years, she had strongly desired to have a baby, but now it seemed a blessing since there was no father for a little one. Was it really a blessing? A child would have been a part of Jonny, a tangible reminder of him. How she longed for that!

Pushing these thoughts from her mind, she paid closer attention to the conversation around her.

More people arrived with food. There was a flat wagon with straw bales in the center and loose straw scattered around. Kara saw a tall man in cowboy hat, jeans, and boots behind a harnessed team of Percherons, holding the reins like he had done it all his life—and probably had. The man expertly hitched the team to the wagon and then asked everyone to get on board. The group started for the wagon but parted like the Red Sea to allow the very pregnant Sandy space and first chance at a seat.

"That's right, folks. Thanks so much. Give Mother Goose room to get on first," said the father-to-be.

"Drew!" Sandy said in an exasperated tone to her husband. Feeling she was past the point of being embarrassed among friends, she waddled as fast as she could to claim a seat on the straw bales. Everyone followed, quickly filling the wagon with bodies. Most wanted a place on the edge of the wagon. Once all were safely seated, the proud Percherons started out at the prompting of the driver. The group sang songs and took part in some good-natured banter as they went merrily down the road.

It was about dusk when the wagon returned to the ranch. Someone had stayed behind to get a fire started for roasting hot dogs. Kara saw logs and lawn chairs circled around the fire and tables set up nearby, weighed down with plenty of food. It appeared as though no one would go hungry from what Kara could see.

Everyone gathered near the tables and bowed their heads as Dennis Cooper, leader of the Bible study, blessed the food. Following the "Amen," everyone helped themselves to the dishes of food. Some volunteered to roast the hot dogs for anyone who did not care to be bothered. Kara, Davey, and Bobbie opted to roast their own. After all, what fun is a wiener roast if you don't do it yourself? Kara was not sure if it was the fresh air or the excellent cooks, but the food was delicious.

Roasting marshmallow was the most fun part, as far as Kara was concerned. She had made certain to bring plenty of those. The best way to cook a marshmallow over an open fire, according to Kara's palate, was to charcoal the plump, fluffy marshmallows with fire. While she was enjoying yet another batch of gooey marshmallows off the stick, Davey approached her with the tall cowboy who had driven the Percherons for the hayride. She was suddenly aware of how foolish she must look with charcoaled, sticky marshmallow all over three of her fingers and her mouth. Some had even managed to get on her nose! Kara hoped the dark shadows would cover the evidence. She would have to inform Davey of the fact that he sometimes had bad timing.

"Kara, I'd like you to meet Cody Ralston. He's the one hosting the wiener roast tonight."

Kara was not sure what to do with her sticky fingers and her mouth full of marshmallows. She quickly swallowed her food and with a red face stammered, "I-uh-I'm pleased to meet you, Cody."

The tall cowboy's eyes twinkled. "Hello, Kara. I'm pleased to meet you too. I hope you're enjoying yourself."

"Yes, very much so. I can't remember when I've had so much fun. Everyone seems so friendly."

"Good. I'm glad to hear it. They really are a great bunch of people. Excuse me, but I have to get my guitar since it appears it's time to start playing for a sing around the campfire." This said, Cody walked away to get his guitar and take his place near the campfire.

Dave suggested they find a place to sit along with everyone else. Bobbie motioned for them to join her on lawn chairs she had brought. Most all joined in the singing. Everyone seemed to blend so well. Kara enjoyed listening to the singers as they harmonized. There was something else too—they sang like they meant it. In a pleasant baritone voice, Cody Ralston led the singing. Even Davey could do a good job of singing. She had never heard her brother sing in public. Growing up, he would sometimes sing with the radio when they were goofing off. It seemed odd that she did not feel misplaced among these people. Maybe that was because they had a sincerity and love for one another.

After a number of songs, Dennis opened his Bible to Psalm 139. In his pleasant voice, he read the scriptures with a power and confidence Kara had never heard anyone use before in her life. Staring into the fire in front of her, the words penetrated her being, seeming to pierce her heart. She had never thought of God being so intimate with a person. Oh, sure, everyone knew God was sitting up there somewhere with His club, ready to point out a person's every wrong.

Listening to Dennis, she realized there really was no getting away from God, which was a scary thought indeed. But as Dennis continued reading, she could hear the verses that spoke also of how God knew her in her mother's womb, knitting the parts together like a potter making something out of clay. The description made God sound like He was a craftsman of sorts who knew individuals before they were born. It was all overwhelming to her and too much to think about. A slight prick of her conscience did nothing for her feelings either. Pushing all thoughts aside, Kara chose instead to pretend she had not heard the scriptures, to stare into the fire and think about nothing in particular.

Unknown to the young woman, Cody Ralston was sitting opposite the fire from her. While the scriptures were read, Cody studied Kara more than listened. He knew from talking to Dave that she was not a Christian and that she was recently widowed. He also realized that he found her quite attractive. He knew he could not let physical attraction get in the way of reasoning. He had made up his mind some time ago when he was saved that he would not join in a union of matrimony with an unbeliever. However, his heart could not help but be stirred with compassion for Kara. The tall cowboy was thinking how she was like a little, lost lamb, seemingly vulnerable and hurting on the inside with the blow life had dealt her. Now that he had met the young woman, he would endeavor to pray more diligently for her. Somehow it made praying for someone easier having met her face to face.

Cody noticed that Kara was one to show emotions on her face. She probably was not aware how her face showed a tangible fear, then a frown, followed by a curious, questioning look. The frown returned and then the face became void of any emotion, like someone had thrown a switch.

Following the reading, Dennis closed with a short prayer, and then it was time for everyone to leave. Someone joked about getting

. . . All Things Become New . . .

to church late in the morning. Dennis warned that there would be no more hayrides unless he saw every last one of them in church the next day.

Cody made it a point to speak to Dave and Kara before they left. He invited them to visit him any time. There were plenty of acres on which to ride horses, if they cared to. Kara had not realized he was part owner of the ranch. She felt even more uncomfortable and foolish as ever as she and Davey walked to the Blazer and took their leave. Cody waved goodbye and she returned the wave with a half-raised arm and a slight smile on her lips. Somehow, she felt better, thinking she was probably making a bigger deal of the marshmallow incident than she should have.

...12

KARA WAS GLAD THE NEXT DAY WAS SUNDAY. SHE NEEDED SOME TIME alone to think. It did not help that she felt unsettled inside. The scriptures Dennis had shared the previous evening kept coming to mind, no matter how hard she tried to empty her head. She was restless as she went from reading a book absentmindedly, to turning on the television, to wandering around the house to see if there was something she had overlooked in doing her chores. Time passed slowly until it was finally time to prepare lunch. Davey would be home soon from church and would be famished. It seemed men were always hungry!

Oh, how her Jonny had loved to eat. He was always active enough that it made no difference on his frame. He just enjoyed food—period. Kara was a decent cook. Many times, Jonny worked alongside her to prepare a meal. She was always a bit envious that he could do a better job of cooking than she could. It was not uncommon for him to prepare a meal for company. Kara loved to try new recipes that complemented the main dish. They had made a good team in the kitchen.

She guessed she should be more creative in Davey's kitchen and impress him. It was Davey, Mom, and Dad who had to suffer as she experimented in the kitchen while growing up, but if she remembered right, there weren't too many disasters. Kara knew she could make a mean stir-fry, among other dishes.

Someone called the young widow's name, bringing her back to the present. Davey came through the door of the kitchen, with Bobbie and Cody in tow. Kara was surprised by the unexpected company, racking her brain in an attempt to remember if her brother had told her they were coming and she had not been paying attention. Rising to the occasion, she added two more place settings at the table, relieved to know she had cooked extra chicken with the intention of having leftovers tomorrow. No matter, she decided.

Both Bobbie and Cody apologized for the intrusion. They mentioned they had offered to bring something for lunch, but Dave had said everything was under control. Kara smiled and assured them it was really not a problem. They appeared relieved by her words.

Bobbie offered to help put the food on the counter. They chose to have a buffet-style meal. In no time, the four were seated at the kitchen table, their full plates before them. Dave blessed the food, and they began light conversation.

Kara was able to study the tall rancher. Today, Cody was wearing a navy-blue-and-white striped western shirt with pearl snaps and a red silk scarf knotted at his throat as well as polished cowboy boots and black jeans.

She had not noticed before his rugged good looks. She thought he should be in one of those magazine advertisements. People were sure to buy the product if a face like his was on the page! Cody was not what one would call dazzling, but there was an attraction. Kara realized how foolish she would appear to those around her if they could read her thoughts. And she a widow of only a few months! She was suddenly ashamed of where her wandering mind was leading—as though a traitor to her late husband's memory!

Hearing her name mentioned, she came out of her dark thoughts to hear Bobbie.

"Are you OK, Kara? You looked like you were miles away and none too happy."

Embarrassed by the attention drawn to her, she mumbled something in reply and pretended to be busy eating. Seeing her discomfort, the others changed the subject to Bobbie's floral business. She and her mother owned and operated the flourishing shop in town. It was a lucrative business and one that Bobbie enjoyed very much.

... Audrey Marr ...

She had a creative flair that she was able to express in floral arrangements. Even the way she had decorated her small apartment spoke volumes of the young woman's talents.

Kara shrugged off her feelings of depression to be more attentive to the conversation around her.

Davey kindly directed a comment to his guest. "Well, I never thought I would move to Montana to become acquainted with a true rancher such as yourself, Cody."

Cody smiled. "I love ranching and feel a certain amount of self-satisfaction working the place. I can't imagine doing anything else with my life."

The others smiled at Cody's remark, noting the sincerity on his face.

"One thing is for sure, Cody," Kara spoke, her eyes sparkling with delight, "you do know how to handle a team of horses. Those draft horses of yours are gorgeous! I would never have believed an animal so large could be so graceful and well-behaved."

"Draft horses are a hobby for Dad and me. We like to use them in local town parades in the summer and in pulling the hay wagon to feed the cattle in the winter. Percherons are a nice breed of horse. Actually, I have always loved horses of any kind. I was one of those children who was riding a horse before I could walk. My dad would take me with him on horseback to check cattle or to do whatever job there was to do for as long as I can remember. We're third-generation ranchers. It's not easy maintaining a ranch these days, with low cattle prices, but the Lord meets our needs every step of the way. Somehow, through God's grace, we do it."

None of what Cody said surprised the others. Neither Davey or Bobbie had been acquainted for a long time with the rancher, but each thought a lot of him and knew Cody to be a hard worker. That he was one who also had a personal relationship with the Lord made him special. The ranch appeared to be very productive and well kept.

"Come to think of it," Cody said, "why don't the three of you consider coming out to the ranch in the near future to ride horseback? A Sunday would suit me best. Then I would be free to take you into the mountains trail riding or to show you the lay of the land on the ranch."

Both Kara and Bobbie got excited about the offer but were a bit concerned about their average riding ability. Cody promised he would give them only what he thought would be a safe mount—tried and proven. They set a date for the following Sunday afternoon. Cody extended the invitation for lunch as well. Then he turned to Kara.

"Kara, I'm sure that speaking for all of us here we would be more than glad to have you attend church service next Sunday."

Kara could read sincerity on the face of the young cowboy. She had not previously noticed how intensely blue Cody's eyes were. A person was immediately drawn to his eyes, appealing and warm. Having met people at the hayride, she guessed she would not be among total strangers, but then again, she was not sure she was ready to be one of those saints either.

"Uh, I-I'm not sure, Cody. I'll think about it, OK? Thanks for asking," she was quick to blurt out, suddenly rising from her chair. "I'd better get busy with clean up."

Everyone offered to help, but the girls quickly banished the men to the living room with the promise that coffee would soon follow. Presently, the women brought steaming cups of gourmet coffee and large slices of apple pie into the living room. It did not take long for the men to eat their share and then some.

Davey asked if they were all up for a board game of some kind. None of the others were familiar with the one he brought out, but all were quick learners. Bobbie was first to win and looked rather smug about it. Davey and Cody gave her a hard time about having played the game before, pretending ignorance. Bobbie fired back a witty answer. Kara could only smile and shake her head in disbelief at the trio.

It was soon time for the guests to take their leave. It had been a fun afternoon and evening. Kara was suddenly feeling weary and took herself to bed. She did not think she should always feel so tired but made the excuse to herself that it must be the events of the past few months. Jonny was never far from her thoughts. It was all too painful for her. Pushing aside memories of her husband, it was not long before Kara was sound asleep.

... 13

THE FOLLOWING WEEK WAS BUSY AT THE AUTO DETAILING SHOP. Dave and Drew had more work than they could handle. Kara proved to be an asset to the business in her office efficiency and her ability in dealing with the public.

On Thursday afternoon, Sandy called and asked to speak to her husband. Drew had a habit of calling his wife often to check on her condition and welfare. Kara had noted a tone of excitement in Sandy's voice. Seeing Drew's face becoming animated as he conversed with his wife, it was not difficult to know the reason.

Slamming down the phone, the father-to-be explained that it was time. Sandy's contractions had finally started and were growing increasingly stronger at shorter intervals. The midwife was already at the house. Before Kara had an opportunity to comment, he was out the door and in his car, driving away. Just then, Dave entered the office to inquire about Drew.

Kara laughed. "He's gone home! That was Sandy on the telephone letting him know it was time. She'd been in labor for a while before she called I'm sure, knowing Drew would be a nervous wreck having to wait too long."

Dave gave a chuckle and went back to work.

... All Things Become New ...

✣ ✣ ✣

At nine o'clock that night, Dave and Kara got a telephone call. It was Drew, breathless with excitement. He and Sandy had a baby girl—seven pounds, nine ounces, and twenty inches long. They had named her Emily Rose Toomey. Mom and baby were fine. It had been an easy delivery, which they were thankful for.

Dave promised he and Kara would stop by soon to see the new arrival and suggested Drew take the next few days off. He kindly reminded the new daddy that he had been a good friend to fill in for him following the death of Jon, and he himself would like to return the favor. Work would not suffer all that much until Monday. Drew was a bit reluctant to agree, but the idea of spending some quality time with his wife and daughter won out in the end.

✣ ✣ ✣

On Saturday afternoon, Davey and Kara went to see the Toomeys. Kara presented Sandy with a gift for Emily before making herself comfortable on the living room recliner.

"Sandy," Kara spoke up, "for a new mom, you look wonderful."

"Thank you, Kara. I'm up and around fine. Having my mother here is spoiling me. I have nothing but time on my hands, even taking the liberty of a nap during the day. Emily is a good baby. I feed her when it's my bedtime, and she wakes only once during the night for a feeding."

The proud papa gave the baby to Kara as they sat around the living room to watch Sandy open the gift. Enclosed in the box was a pink dress with lots of lace for the baby to wear when she was older. Ruffled leotards and a hair bow were included. Sandy thanked Kara and Dave for the gift. She had no larger clothes for the baby as of yet.

Baby Emily won the hearts of all with her jet-black hair and long, dark eyelashes like her mother. On a scale of one to ten, everyone agreed she was a ten. Drew's chest swelled as he tenderly held his daughter while everyone visited.

Sandy's mother entered the living room and introduced herself. Rose Gardner was an attractive woman. Kara could see from where Sandy and the baby had inherited their dark complexion.

There was a definite resemblance. Rose informed the guests she was there to help out around the house for a few days and to take advantage of her first grandchild. She served everyone coffee and cake, joining in the conversation.

Eventually, Davey stood, advising Kara that they needed to get home.

Kara spoke as she prepared to leave. "Drew and Sandy, your daughter is beautiful! I'm so glad for you both. Maybe I'll stop by again next week sometime, Sandy, if that's all right with you. I'll be sure to call first."

"Please do, Kara. I'd love it!" Sandy said as she embraced her and walked them to the door. "Thank you two for stopping by and for the gift."

Dave and Kara did some errands while in town. They were both excited about horseback riding the next day. Since Kara had only hiking shoes and tennis shoes, they shopped in a western wear store for a pair of comfortable footwear for riding. The sales clerk assured Kara that the style she had chosen was a popular one among western women. Pleased with her purchases, she opted for an Aussie-style hat also. Davey teased her about turning into a true Montanan if she was not careful. Kara mentioned that was not a bad idea. She was beginning to appreciate the new friends she had made while in Montana and felt they could be friends for life.

Upon Kara's suggestion, they went to an Italian restaurant—her treat.

✜   ✜   ✜

Sunday morning proved to be a sunny, pleasant day. Shortly after Kara had begun working for her brother, he had offered her the use of his small pickup truck. It would be her means of transportation while in Montana. She was touched by Davey's sensitivity to understand her need for some independence.

Kara had suggested to Davey that she meet him at Bobbie's place, which was in town. They could ride out to Cody's ranch together. Davey felt bad that she would not take Cody's invitation to church seriously. All he could do was pray. Kara was a grown woman, and it was out of his hands.

. . . All Things Become New . . .

Kara prepared for the anticipated adventure with care. She dressed in a light denim shirt and blue jeans. The jeans were a bit trying to zip, which concerned her. To her knowledge, she had not changed her eating habits. If anything, she had eaten less and had possibly lost a few pounds due to the stress of the past months. After expertly braiding her light brown hair into a French braid and tying a blue bandana on the end of the braid, she donned her new western boots and readied to leave. The problem with her waistline would wait. She set her mind on enjoying the day.

True to her word, Kara met Bobbie and Dave at the appointed time. The girls were breathless with excitement about the prospect of horseback riding. In no time they were at the ranch. Cody greeted the trio as they entered the house. The aroma from the kitchen made everyone's mouths water. It smelled like Mexican food.

When lunch was ready to be served, Cody escorted the guests to the dining room. An older woman with a platter of homemade tamales entered from the kitchen, her husband following, carrying dishes of beans and rice. The guests were not aware of how many hours Rita Ralston had spent in preparing the meal, or they would have felt even more honored by the dishes served them. Cody introduced his parents to Kara, who had never met them.

Rita and Martin Ralston were pleasant people. Rita appeared to have Mexican blood in her, with her dark eyes and complexion. Martin had blue eyes and fair hair, which was slightly gray at the temples. He had the build of a younger man—tall and slim, with broad shoulders. Kara glanced over at the son to note that he had the dark hair and complexion of his mother, inheriting the blue eyes from his dad, of course. Cody had a strong jaw, which spoke of a possible stubborn streak, and laugh lines at the corners of his eyes, probably due to all the hours spent outdoors. She realized the young cowboy stood an inch or so taller than her brother. Cody was slightly leaner but had broad shoulders like Davey's.

Martin said the blessing over the food and then everyone helped themselves. The mouthwatering dishes were a treat to all. Mr. and Mrs. Ralston proved to be gracious hosts, desiring to know their guests better.

Rita smiled at Kara as she questioned her. "So, Kara, how do you like Montana? From what I understand, you had never been to the Big Sky State until a short while ago."

Kara returned the smile, warmed by the woman's kind eyes. "I have been enjoying Montana immensely. Everyone I have met so far has been nothing but warm and friendly. I do believe the air out here is clearer than back east and definitely crisp this time of year."

"I'm glad, dear, that Montana and its people have been good to you. You have had some difficult times, and I would not want to see more added to your small shoulders. I'm truly sorry about the loss of your husband."

Kara knew Rita was genuine, as tears pooled in the woman's brown eyes. "Thank you, Mrs. Ralston. I appreciate your sincerity."

Martin decided he had better change the topic of conversation before all the women were crying. "Cody, you should tell these good people about some of your daring feats as a boy."

Cody was quite the storyteller and glad to oblige his father. He soon had everyone laughing. It appeared he had been some character growing up, always finding himself in trouble for one reason or another. His sister suffered much at his hands and would have gladly told anyone who would listen, but she was presently away competing at a rodeo barrel-racing event.

After the meal, the guests made certain to compliment the cook before Cody escorted them outside to the corrals, where four horses were already saddled and tied to the hitching post. Three dogs accompanied them—a black Labrador and a pair of Australian Shepherds. Cody stopped to fondly pet each dog and talk to them.

Looking to his guests, he explained, "The black Lab's name is Pepper. She's great company for me and likes to jump in the back of my truck and go wherever I'm going. The other two are cow dogs. Australian Shepherds have stubby tails and are a great breed of working dog to have on the ranch. They save me a lot of time and energy by helping move cattle to different pastures and such. I can only be one place at once on a horse or on foot. I give these dogs a verbal command to go to the right or left behind the herd to keep the cattle bunched and moving. They make my work easy."

Nearing the horses at the hitching rail, Kara could see beyond to the corrals where several other horses were held. She was excited to think about horseback riding. She was going to have a lot to share with her friends back east. She could already picture the look of envy on their faces when she told them this or that about her stay in Montana.

... All Things Become New ...

Cody advised Bobbie to mount Tar Baby, a black mare with two white stockings. Kara climbed on a sorrel mare called Penny. Dave was given a white gelding by the name of Frank. Cody rode Buddy. They set out for a destination that their leader had in mind. The ranch itself was open, with a few evergreen trees scattered on the gently rolling hills, which came up against the base of the mountain range. Following a well-worn path into the foothills, the riders noted the coolness traveling among the trees.

Along with the pleasant, pungent odor of pines, the exhilarating, fresh air and the quietness of the wooded area seemed to seep into a person's being. It felt wonderful to relax and relish their surroundings! They loved every minute of their adventure. Cody refused to explain where they were going, encouraging them to enjoy the ride.

With no warning, they came to the edge of a clearing; a lush, green meadow spread before them. The three riders looked with mouths gaping at the sight while Cody observed them, pleased with their reaction. In the meadow stood a herd of a hundred elk or more, some with calves by their sides. They had been resting in the late afternoon but had gotten up at the sound of human voices. They weren't spooked but were uneasy, undecided what they should do.

Having never seen elk before, the women were speechless with the wonder of it all. Davey had hunted elk, but it was a sight to behold so many in their natural environment, looking somewhat at ease with the horses present. The cow elk made mewing noises among themselves, communicating to their young and one another. Some in the elk herd were mildly curious about the horses, venturing toward the four, thinking they were possibly one of their kind.

Kara was first to speak in a loud whisper, breaking the silence, "I've never seen elk before, except on television or in a picture. This is so awesome! Cody, this was definitely worth the ride! I'm so glad you brought us here."

Bobbie and Davey quickly added their approval too.

Time seemed to stand still as they continued to watch the large, dark creatures move about. There were some bull elk among the herd, each proudly bearing a large rack on his head as a king would a crown of jewels.

... Audrey Marr ...

Cody finally suggested they start back to the ranch before it got too late. Taking a different route back, the riders arrived at the ranch long before they wanted the adventure to end. It had been a rewarding day for them all. Cody was always pleased to take people on a tour of the ranch that they might enjoy what the Lord had so graciously given him and his family. The guests realized it all came about with a lot of hard work. To be sure, the Ralstons had proven they were good stewards. The young rancher invited his guests to refresh themselves with a glass of iced tea and perhaps a sandwich before leaving as they stiffly dismounted the horses.

Martin was awaiting their arrival and gladly offered to tend to the horses so Cody was able to walk the trio to the house. Rita had been expecting them and considered it no trouble at all in getting a few things together for a light meal. About the time everyone was ready to be seated, Cody's father returned from the corrals to take his place at the table also. After the hearty meal they had eaten earlier, no one believed they could eat much. Maybe it was the fresh air and activity of the day, but eat they did. Rita and Martin Ralston were once again their warm and friendly selves, causing Kara to relax and thoroughly enjoy her time with them. It was as though she had known the Ralston family forever.

Martin smiled and asked his guests in general, "So, what do the three of you think of the Lazy R Ranch—what little you saw of it anyway?"

All three faces lit with delight. Bobbie spoke up, her blue eyes sparkling. "It was gorgeous! I could have stayed in that mountain meadow forever!"

Kara's green eyes were huge with wonder as she looked first to Martin and then to Rita. "I had never seen elk before. It was awesome! And to think I actually saw them in their own habitat. So many of my friends are going to be green with envy back east when they find out about my adventure on horseback. I can't wait to tell them either!"

"It really was a privilege and a special treat, Mr. Ralston," Dave stated. Turning to Cody, he continued, "Thanks so much for taking the time to take us greenhorns out for a tour of the place."

"It was my pleasure, Dave. Maybe we'll do it again sometime."

Talk continued around the table. When conversation waned, Davey glanced at his watch and stated that it was time to leave. Days were long in June, and the time of day could be deceiving.

The Ralstons walked their guests to the vehicle. Martin gave each of them a warm smile. "Don't be strangers now that you know where we live, all right? Feel at liberty to visit us any time."

"Yes, please do!" Rita heartily agreed. "Don't wait for an invite. We enjoy having company. This time of year the visitors slack off a bit with the nice weather and all."

Before entering the Blazer, the trio promised to visit again. The three Ralstons waved as the departing guests drove away.

Contentment swept over Kara as she crawled into bed that night, reflecting on the satisfying, full day. She could not help being glad she had made the decision to come to Montana to be with her brother. With an arm stretched across the empty space beside her, she fell into a restful sleep, feeling like she could sink to the bottom of the bed in her weariness.

...14

T HE DAYS TOOK ON A SET AND PREDICTABLE PATTERN FOR KARA IN THE weeks that followed. That suited her fine. Often, she was so busy she did not have time to dwell on her loss, though she thought of Jonny often enough. The young widow was able to fill her extra time with visits to Sandy and little Emily Rose or to Bobbie at her floral shop. Since she did not have to work a full day during the week, she was able to spend time getting to know the two women. There was a feeling of bonding and kindred spirit with them.

The small garden flourished under her intense care through the weeks. From the proceeds of the garden, Kara was often able to make a stir-fry or to serve fresh vegetables at a meal. It was fun to watch the flowers bloom and enhance the beauty of her brother's lawn too. Kara found it all very rewarding.

One Saturday morning, Kara had taken the liberty to sleep in. She and Davey had been out late the night before with Bobbie. Not being a night person anyway, Kara went to bed feeling especially weary that night. As she awoke, she stretched, having enjoyed a restful night. The feather bed felt delightful as she rolled onto her stomach to relax and give her sleepy self time to wake up. She had never given any thought about it before, but she suddenly noticed a tenderness to her chest and a different feeling, a firmness, in her lower abdomen.

. . . All Things Become New . . .

Struck by a sudden thought, Kara bolted upright in bed, shocked with the realization of what it all could mean. She had worked around numerous women for several years, listening and sharing in conversations with them. But this! This was something she had never expected in her wildest dreams—after all these years! Her face drained of all color as her mind whirled with possibilities. She stumbled into the bathroom to wash her face and try to clear her head. This couldn't be—it just couldn't be!

Kara returned to her room to plop onto the bed. Unable to absorb the knowledge of what she suspected any longer, she curled into a fetal position, hugging a pillow to herself. She gave in to the torrent of tears and wept as she had not done for some time, wishing more than ever that her Jonny was beside her.

✢   ✢   ✢

The house was quiet when Davey came home in the early afternoon. He had mentioned to Kara that they should do some shopping once he was finished working. She had agreed to the idea; she always enjoyed browsing in the stores. He went to the kitchen, assuming she was there, but did not find her. After making a quick sandwich, he decided to seek her out. Maybe she was outside puttering in the garden. He worried that she was still doing too much as it was. She always looked tired, although she never complained.

She was not in the garden. Fear filled him as he considered the fact that she could be ill and still in bed. Anxious to know her whereabouts, he ran into the house, coming to an abrupt halt in the kitchen at his sister's appearance. Her face was blotched, her eyes swollen and red-rimmed as though she had been crying for some time.

Davey was aghast. "Kar, are you OK?"

Unable to speak, her arms hanging loosely at her sides, his sister could only give a helpless shrug of her shoulders before covering her face with her hands and weeping.

Davey hurried to her, embracing her as if to protect her from unseen forces. He felt helpless to know what to do or say, not knowing what the problem was. *This must be serious*, he thought. He began to silently pray for his sister. *Lord, whatever the problem is, help Kara to surrender to You. She's so needy and doesn't realize it. Please give me the wisdom to help her. I love her, but I know Your love for her is greater. Help me to know what to say or do for her in Jesus' name. Amen.*

Davey continued to hold his sister firmly in his arms. After her sobs had quieted, he asked, "Do you want to talk about it?"

Finding comfort in her brother's arms, she nodded her head as she rested against his broad chest. With a heavy sigh and shudder, she blurted out the words she had a hard time believing herself. "I think I'm pregnant!" This brought another rush of tears.

Davey was stunned. "Pregnant?" he questioned as he moved his sister to arm's length so he could look into her eyes and then inadvertently to her flat stomach. He knew this was not some funny joke, but it was difficult to take in. Poor Kara! Davey suggested they sit down in the living room to absorb the news and talk.

Davey numbly sat next to Kara on the sofa, drawing her into his big loving arms for a few moments. Quick to recover, he spoke a sudden thought, "Wow! I would've never dreamt this one! And to think I'm going to be an uncle! Oh, Kar, Jon would've been so happy. He mentioned from time to time that he hoped to be a dad some day. He was always patient and good with kids."

Upon hearing this, Kara removed herself from her brother's embrace to stare at him in disbelief. How could he be talking about the news as if it were a great event? All she knew was that the baby would be without a father—a man who would have been a wonderful father. She was missing her husband more than ever with the thoughts of a baby—something she had desired to give Jonny ever since they had said their marriage vows.

"It's OK, Kar. We'll make it through this. In a matter of months, the baby will be here. That is assuming you are going to stay here with me. There's plenty of room here for the three of us."

"Oh, Davey, maybe I'm assuming too much. Maybe it's not really true. What I need to do is have a pregnancy test done."

"Hey, don't they have those at-home tests you can do? I'll bet they're dependable. At least that's what the television commercials say."

"Maybe you're right. It's worth a try."

"Yeah, but I think you should go to bed and take a nap. You look like you've been put through the wringer. Would you mind if I call Bobbie and let her know about the possibility of me being an uncle?

"No, that would be fine. Bobbie is turning out to be a very good friend."

Kara didn't need any prodding to go to bed. It seemed a wise thing to do. Davey mentioned the fact that it would not be too late to do some shopping once she had rested.

After looking in on his sister a short while later to be certain she actually slept, he spent some time in serious prayer for her. He felt compelled to make a few phone calls to request prayer for this unexpected turn of events, but he knew that until they were certain of the pregnancy, Kara would not be comfortable with anyone except Bobbie knowing. A baby of all things! It did not take long to warm to the idea. To have a little niece or nephew call him Uncle Davey sounded good. It kind of had a nice ring to it.

✣   ✣   ✣

Following a restful nap, Kara was able to think more rationally. Her emotions had seemingly gotten the best of her with the idea of an unexpected pregnancy. She was hesitant about getting on with life though. Well, it's not like she was alone in this. She knew she would have the support of not only her brother but also Jonny's family. Wouldn't Dad and Mom Madison be surprised to get the news they were going to be grandparents! She supposed the best move to make was to purchase a home pregnancy test kit and see if what she suspected was true. One day at a time; one event at a time. Thoughts of having Jonny's baby made her feel that she yet had a part of her belated husband with her. If she were pregnant, she hoped it was a boy and that he looked like his dad. It would seem fitting, considering the circumstances.

Kara suddenly felt overwhelmed and weary with it all. She guessed she had to get used to the idea. Just the fact that Jonny should have been with her to celebrate the coming baby made her heart heavy. After a shower, she felt better and decided to put on her best smile and find her brother.

It was not difficult to find him. Failing to stay awake while reading the newspaper, Davey was catnapping on the living room sofa. Kara allowed him to sleep as she gazed upon his sleeping form with tenderness. He was so good to her and good for her. Like a cuddly teddy bear, he was so loving too. If there were a God in heaven, He had certainly blessed her to give her such a brother.

Kara chose one of the chairs to sit in and browse through a magazine. In minutes, Davey awoke to peer at her sleepily.

"Well, at least you look better, Kar," he said in a gravelly voice.

Kara rewarded him with a smile. "I've decided it could be a lot worse for me. I'm fortunate to have the loving support of so many, including a wonderful brother in particular."

Davey grinned with satisfaction at the compliment. "I love you, Kar. I have to be honest in saying that I think a baby is a wonderful blessing. It could be one of the best things ever to happen to you."

He sat up quickly on the sofa, excitement rising in him as he continued. "The Lord is good! Think of the pleasure a baby can bring. And," he added, with a raised index finger to make his point, "he or she will be a part of Jon too, meaning he'll live on in that baby."

Kara released a heavy sigh. "Maybe before we jump to any more conclusions, we had better get to town and do some shopping."

This said, her brother moved to put on his shoes. He mentioned they could get something to eat in town, too, since neither of them felt up to cooking.

✤ ✤ ✤

Kara awoke early the next morning, thinking how a few hours would tell the truth. She followed the directions on the home kit and waited. The test was positive. This fact made all doubts dissipate, and she was faced with the reality of her situation. She walked out of the bathroom to lean against the bedroom wall, slumping to the floor to hold her folded legs against herself. A baby! She was really going to have a baby! After so many disappointing months and years of waiting, only to have her hopes crushed again and again.

Jonny had been so understanding and patient about everything. He was willing to wait, assuring her they were both young yet. A few weeks before his death, he had shared with her the story of Abraham and Sarah, which he had been reading about in the Bible. All she could think was that she hoped she did not have to be that old before she had a baby. If he was trying to console her, he was not doing a very good job of it! Thinking about this brought a smile to her lips. Dear Jonny! Oh, how she missed him! She could envision the excitement he would have shown at the news of a coming baby. With a loud whoop, he would have picked her up to whirl her around the room in his glee.

A gentle rap sounded on her bedroom door, bringing Kara out of her pensive mood. Davey popped his head around the door. "Well?"

Kara smiled and nodded her head.

With a whoop, Davey was in the room, sweeping his sister off the floor to gently whirl her around the room, reminding her of all the fun things he would do with the baby and what a great uncle he would be.

He wasn't Jonny, but she couldn't fault him for that. One would have thought he was going to be a daddy the way he was acting! It was just like her brother to be able to make it all seem good and right somehow. She laughed at her brother's excitement, returning his hug. Yes, everything was going to be OK after all.

...15

DAVEY HAD DECIDED IT WAS IMPORTANT FOR HIM TO SPEND TIME WITH his sister rather than go to church that day. Kara had insisted she would be fine, but with his persistence she relented.

The two spent time talking about their childhood memories, parents, and Jonny. It was a turning point for the young widow. Sharing her thoughts and feeling seemed to release something within her. If she had considered it, she would have noticed a tenderness that had been gradually seeping into her being. It was the gentle touch of the Shepherd wooing her to Himself. Even though she was not aware of His love for her, the Lord was holding her to Himself, caring intimately about all that she was going through.

✢ ✢ ✢

A concerned Bobbie came to visit at two o'clock that afternoon. Unknown to Kara, the young widow was the topic of many conversations between Bobbie and Dave. Through the weeks, Kara had become dear to Bobbie. She shared Dave's burden that Kara might come to accept the Lord as her Savior. Kara was like the older sister she had never had.

... All Things Become New ...

Being an only child, Bobbie had never had the privilege of knowing what it was like to have another sibling around. She had always been a friendly, outgoing person, never lacking for friends, but she had never been intimate with any of them. For some reason, she had been drawn to Kara from the beginning, secretly hoping to meet Kara. Dave had spoken about his sister with such love and adoration. Bobbie was confident that the Lord was going to save Kara if she would ever stop running from Him and run to Him.

Davey and Kara were pleased to see her.

Bobbie seated herself in a chair across from the two at their prompting. "How are you doing, Kara? There are a lot of people concerned for your welfare. After meeting you at the hayride, folks were hoping to see more of you. Dave called me last night, worried and requesting prayer for you."

Kara was moved by her friend's concern as well as embarrassed that so much attention had been drawn to her. Did Davey's entire church know what a basket case she had been?

Noticing Kara's look of horror and understanding where her thoughts were leading, Davey quickly spoke up. "Everything is fine, Kar. The people in my church are like an extended family. I was concerned a great deal about you yesterday but respected your right to some kind of privacy. You can relax, OK?"

Greatly relieved by Davey's words, Kara sheepishly spoke up. "I'm sorry, Bobbie, if I caused anyone concern. I hadn't meant to alarm you. I'm fine. Really. It just takes some getting used to the idea, you know—a baby and all."

Bobbie's eyes grew wide with the realization of what Kara said. "Then it's really true? You are going to have a baby? I mean, Dave mentioned it on the phone last night, but I wasn't sure he knew what he was talking about. I thought he might have misunderstood you since you were so upset and all."

In mock horror, with his hand over his heart, Davey blurted, "What say you, dear Bobbie? That I am one to exaggerate on occasion, especially when it comes to knowing things about my own sister?"

Now it was Bobbie's turn to be embarrassed. Kara looked on the scene with a smile, her affection for her friend clearly showing on her face.

"Well, no—uh—I mean . . ."

"Don't let this guy get to you, Bobbie," Kara said, a twinkle in her eyes. "He's trying to give you a hard time about it all. I used a home testing kit and the result was positive. Along with some obvious symptoms, I believe it's safe to say that I'm certain I am pregnant."

"Oh, Kara! I'm so happy for you! What a blessing this baby will be to you. To think that it will be a part of your Jonny too. The Lord knows what He's doing. I thought Dave was assuming a lot, talking about what a great uncle he was going to be to the baby."

Kara nodded her head in agreement. "Did you have lunch, Bobbie? There are fixings for sandwiches in the frig. We haven't eaten yet ourselves. Just being lazy today, remembering and getting sentimental about the events of the past."

Saying this, Kara led the group to the kitchen where the main topic of conversation to follow was the coming baby.

✣ ✣ ✣

Kara made it a point to call her in-laws. Jonathan and Alice Madison were elated with the news once the initial shock wore off. They too had hoped for some time that their Jon and Kara would have a family, but the possibility had died along with their son. After making small talk, the more practical side took over. Alice suggested that Kara see a doctor to confirm the pregnancy and begin prenatal care.

"What will you do now that you are going to have a baby? Would you consider coming back here to stay with us during your confinement? Maybe when the baby is born you can decide if you want to live on your own or not."

"I haven't decided about anything, Alice. The realization of actually having a baby hasn't quite settled in my mind. I feel fine and I am enjoying the job I have at Davey's shop. You know me. I can't sit around getting huge with a baby and not being active. The people out here have been wonderful. To tell you the truth, I've been having a great time, all things considered. Davey has been good for me."

"Well, dear, you know that we would love to have you. You are always welcome here. When do you think the baby is due?"

"I have no idea since I haven't been to a doctor. I took the home pregnancy test just this morning to confirm that I am with child."

"Would you mind if we perhaps came out there for a visit soon?"

"No, of course not. It would be great to see you again. I do miss you all."

After discussing a possible date to visit and updating Kara on happenings with the family—Jonny's brothers in particular—the conversation ended.

As she hung up the telephone, Kara wondered why she felt hesitant to return east, to her home. She was not sure she could return to her house, a place filled with memories of her Jonny, who was no longer with her. Starting afresh in Montana appealed to her at the present. Bobbie and Sandy had become so dear to her, and Davey was more precious than ever. It was surprising what a few months could do.

At least she did not feel pressured to make a hasty decision since Davey had repeatedly assured her that a baby was an exciting affair and he would like nothing better than to share his home and heart with the little one. Davey had loved her late husband like a brother, but then that was Davey. He had always been affectionate like their parents, yet since professing Christ, he seemed even more so.

Maybe a walk would do her good. She had excused herself earlier to allow Davey and Bobbie some privacy, even making a subtle suggestion that they go for a drive or get some exercise by taking a walk. The two had chosen the latter and were off on one of the many logging roads. Since she knew Davey's favorite walking paths, she made certain to go in the opposite direction. The days were long and the sun shone warm and bright on this particular Sunday. It did feel good to be alive and to breathe deeply of the fresh air, even if being without a loved one was painful.

... 16

News traveled fast of the expected baby. Kara was not certain it was good or bad, but she took the well wishes in stride. The pregnancy was beginning to affect her in a positive way. She found herself thinking constantly about the baby growing inside of her, wondering if she carried a boy or girl, what he or she would look like, what preparations she would have to make for its arrival. It would have been fun to choose baby furniture and clothes with Jonny beside her, planning their future together.

Yet, if she had to choose a substitute, her brother fit the bill. Most conversations with him were about the baby. There was no hurry to reach a decision concerning the birthplace of the baby—east or west. Following a discussion with Sandy regarding her pregnancy and birthing experience, Kara was interested in talking with Sandy's midwife. To have a baby at home was a totally different concept, and she was not sure how her in-laws would react toward the idea. First she would visit the midwife, and then she could make some decisions. It was a start.

✥   ✥   ✥

Kara was able to make an appointment for the following week with the midwife who had delivered little Emily Toomey. Joyce

Andrews was a woman of nearly forty who had had extensive training for the role. She had prepared with a two-year course in midwifery, delivered over two hundred babies in her career, and had borne four children of her own. All were born at home under the supervision of another midwife. Kara felt the woman was definitely qualified for the job.

Joyce was a warm, friendly person, one whom Kara felt at ease with after conversing only a few moments. She professed to be a Christian, but Kara would not hold that against her. Joyce considered midwifery a ministry to others, both spiritually and physically. She made certain to share Christ during her visits with the mothers-to-be, never offensively but with love, sincerity and an eagerness to share her testimony about the love of Christ and the plan of salvation.

Following a few preliminary questions and a simple examination, Joyce discussed exercise, nutrition, and what to expect in the months ahead in the way of bodily changes and the development of the baby. She estimated the due date for the arrival of the baby to be December 30. The midwife then shared Psalm 139:13–16, expressing how we are all fearfully and wonderfully made by an awesome God. Kara could not refute that. She had given that very scripture passage a lot of thought since hearing it the night of the hayride.

After a glass of herbal iced tea, Joyce took her leave. The midwife had been very encouraging to Kara and had said she would be happy to follow up with prenatal care as well as the delivery of the baby should Kara decide to stay in Montana and opt for a home birth.

Kara had some serious thinking to do. She felt obligated to reach a decision at least about where to live. Nothing definite came to her. Feeling restless, she did some household chores, put dinner in the oven, and went for a walk, hoping to clear her mind.

Over dinner that night, Davey asked his sister if she would like to go camping over the weekend. Cody wanted to go on a fishing trip before the mad rush to put up hay for the ranch. He felt the ranch could survive a few days without him and had invited Davey to go along. After some conversation, the men had decided to invite Bobbie and Kara also.

. . . Audrey Marr . . .

Cody's father was always after him about working too much, so he had decided to take advantage of his father's suggestion. Martin had also voiced his concern to Cody on occasion that time was passing and he was hoping to eventually become a grandfather. Cody had to admit that several women at church and in the area seemed nice enough, but none had interested him in the least. In the past few weeks, a pair of emerald green eyes belonging to one particular young widow had come to mind several times. The tall rancher knew it was wrong for him to consider Kara. Unless she came to the Lord, there would not be a completeness in their marriage. He guessed he was willing to wait; time would tell. He knew through conversations with Dave that Kara may choose to pack up and return to her home back east. The young rancher spent a great deal of time in prayer for the young woman, as did several other people. If he didn't know better, he was sure that Kara seemed happy being in the west with her brother. She was a congenial person, one who was liked immediately by everyone who met her. However, only the Lord could soften the heart.

Being an outdoorsy person, Kara was delighted with the idea of camping. She could hardly wait for Friday evening, yet she could not deny her concern about riding a horse in her condition. However, Joyce had advised that as long as she did not do a lot of bumpy, fast riding she should be fine, using caution. After all, Kara had ridden a horse before she knew she was pregnant.

Cody had suggested they leave the ranch about 7 P.M. on horseback for a campsite he had in mind. With the daylight hours long, it was not an impossible feat. Cody would collect the food and necessary gear at the auto body shop on Friday. Then he would saddle the horses and ready the packhorse for travel. Once the workday was over, the three guests would have only to get to the ranch and take leave.

Friday morning, Bobbie entered the shop, with the items she was to provide, breathless with excitement. A pro at camping, she had organized the necessary meals and snacks with the understanding that Cody was responsible for the camping gear. She could not stay long to chat since she had to open the floral shop soon, but she was able to clear up a few last-minute details with Kara and Davey before leaving.

... All Things Become New ...

Later that morning, Cody entered the office. A cheery Kara greeted him. She seemed like a breath of fresh air to the young cowboy. He could not imagine living through such a tragedy as she had experienced. He knew she surely had her moments, but for the most part the widow appeared to be adjusting. Maybe the pregnancy had something to do with it. Kara looked radiant this morning; her green eyes sparkled and her face became animated as she spoke of the outing. She had never tented out and was looking forward to the experience. Her only previous experience had been spending time at a hunting cabin the Madison family owned. In the mountains about fifty miles from town, the cabin came with most of the comforts of home.

Kara invited Cody to take a seat by the desk and enjoy a cup of coffee. Davey wanted to speak to him concerning work he needed done on a ranch truck. Being Friday, the shop was surprisingly slow. The bookwork was caught up, so there was only the telephone to answer and customers to deal with. Cody noticed the woman's efficiency and charisma; she seemed a natural with the public. The rancher wondered if she would consider going out to dinner with him sometime, provided he could get up the nerve to ask.

Slow down, buddy, Cody told himself. *You'd better be thinking of taking her to a Bible study instead!*

He liked being with this young woman more than he cared to admit and told himself he was going to enjoy the weekend. He also realized it could be difficult to keep his thoughts in order where Kara Madison was concerned. He had best not entertain any romantic notions as he noted the wedding band on Kara's finger. Dave and Bobbie, always being a lot of fun, would be the distraction he could use and need.

Dave entered the office, interrupting his thoughts. After the men discussed the ranch truck, Kara took charge to set up an appointment. With no further reason to be there, Cody excused himself and packed his pickup truck with the food and their personal belongings.

Closing the shop later that afternoon, Davey met Kara and Bobbie at a local restaurant for dinner. There was no rush to be to the ranch, so the trio enjoyed the meal and conversation.

It was 6:45 P.M. when the three arrived at the Lazy R Ranch. True to his word, Cody was prepared to leave. After making small talk with Rita and Martin, the trio excused themselves. As they mounted the horses, another rider came around the corner of the barn. It was Hannah Ralston, Cody's sister. At twenty-two years of age, she was already in the running for the state championship in barrel racing. A sudden change of plans included her on the camp out.

Hannah favored her father in looks with her fair skin, blond hair, and blue eyes. Kara took an immediate liking to her. Davey and Bobbie were already acquainted with her since they attended the same church. It appeared the Ralstons all had a sense of humor; they seemed a solid family in every sense of the word. They were dedicated, hard workers who also knew how to have a good time and enjoy life. It was going to be a fun weekend for sure.

Keeping a steady pace, the riders arrived at the campsite by 9 P.M. The men agreed to set up the tents while the women went in search of firewood and stones for building a fire. Bobbie and Hannah fussed over Kara, not allowing her to carry any heavy objects. She was given the job of gathering kindling instead. It seemed no time at all before the camp was organized and they were relaxing around a fire. They placed logs in lieu of chairs near the fire.

"So, Cody, what do you have in mind for tomorrow?" Hannah asked.

"Well, I do believe fishing in Trapper Lake should be a priority. One can't go camping without going fishing and eating the catch, to my way of thinking. I thought we could do some exploring on horseback; we'll be able to cover more territory that way. Neither you nor I have been up here since last year. I thought we should share with our friends a favorite place of ours, if you understand what I'm saying?"

Hannah's eyes sparkled in the growing darkness. "I never tire of that place myself!" Looking to each of the newcomers, she said, "I think all of you will like the place Cody has in mind, as well as the fishing. But for now, did anyone pack a fun snack we could eat?"

Kara suggested they roast marshmallows. She had made sure she packed plenty for that very purpose. Bobbie brought the marshmallows out of the cooler along with iced tea to enjoy. Cody had managed to safely pack his guitar, which he soon began strumming. The group sang simple songs about the love of God; some Kara remembered from the hayride party. Since she did not know the words, she was content to hum along. There was a time when she would have been offended to have to listen to the songs, but now they seemed pleasant to her. Maybe the reason was she personally knew all those around the fire and they had become dear to her. Even Hannah could be seen, not as a hypocrite, but as true-blue. All of them sang like they meant it. They had shown her nothing but love and acceptance. No, she really did not mind at all.

✧ ✧ ✧

The women shared one tent. Each had a mat and a sleeping bag.

Davey explained to Kara that should she need to go out, she must tell someone. With wilderness all around, there were bears, mountain lions and rattlesnakes to avoid. At least in the cool nights the snakes were not a worry. Then she should take Cody's black Lab, Pepper, for company. Cody's dogs were his companions, and he had allowed Pepper to come along for the dog's sake as well as theirs. Kara assured her brother she would be fine and promised she would do as he said.

Being pregnant was a joy to Kara daily, once she had gotten over the initial shock. Even though she was not showing yet, the little one seemed to be growing down, placing pressure often in an area she wished he wouldn't. This made for more frequent trips "out" than she cared for. It was almost embarrassing! The other two women had each taken a turn with Kara and were sleeping soundly when her discomfort again forced her from her sleeping bag. Given time, it would not be so bad, Sandy Toomey had comforted her, but at the moment it did not help matters. She could not wait much longer!

As quiet as she could, she crept out of the tent with a flashlight. Softly calling for the dog, she nearly jumped out of her skin when a cold, wet nose touched her hand from behind. Pepper blended well with the darkness. Kara was glad for the light to know she had not encountered a wild animal. Taking several steps towards the nearby trees, Kara suddenly realized the dog was no longer with her. Shining the light around as she called for the dog brought no results. She guessed the dog had been too tired to follow. Well, she was not a baby. She could handle going into the woods alone, keeping the camp in sight.

Finished with her task, Kara groped for the flashlight she had turned off. She was sure she had put it within easy reach of her right hand. Grumbling to herself about her stupidity at 3 A.M., she finally found the flashlight and stumbled out of the bushes, tripping over a tangle of weeds that brought her painfully to her hands and knees, scraping them a little. It was not a dangerous fall, just a clumsy one. She was thankful no one else was around to notice how foolish she must look. With a sigh, she brushed herself off and started walking toward the camp.

Shining the flashlight ahead of her, she never saw the half-exposed tree root hidden in a clump of grass. With just a pair of thongs on her bare feet, the sharp end of the splintered root shoved between her foot and the sandal, cutting a groove along part of her big toe and the ball of her right foot. With a sharp cry of pain escaping her lips, she quickly stooped to grab her foot. Sitting down, she gently pulled her foot away from the root. Shining the flashlight, she could see the blood streaming from the wound. She tried to stem the flow with finger pressure. Biting her lower lip against the pain, she did not believe the cut to be a bad one, but it was painful nonetheless. Hearing her name called softly in the darkness, Kara looked up to see someone approaching with a flashlight.

Cody was obviously scared by seeing the young woman on the ground. His look was one of concern and worry, feeling the full weight of his responsibility upon observing her like that. It was clear that Kara was a real trooper who was attempting to be brave.

"Kara! Are you OK?"

Embarrassed to be caught in such a foolish predicament, she could only nod her head, all the while holding her foot. It was all she could do to keep from crying about everything—the pain and her discomfort. She was certain that Cody would never ask her to go on another campout after this, especially since she was pregnant and all.

Cody noticed Kara holding her foot. He was not sure the extent of the injury and thought it best to get her back to camp. Scooping her gently in his arms with ease born of years of physical labor, he quietly spoke words of encouragement. It was clear she was in some pain.

Kara had not expected Cody to take such action and could only bury her head against his chest. She could feel the cords of muscle underneath her and was aware of his nearness. She hoped no one else was awake to see all of this.

In no time at all, they were back at the campsite. Cody gently placed her on a log and went to get the first-aid kit he kept in his gear. Kara tried to calm herself, thinking she was making too much of everything. The rancher promptly returned with the kit in hand. He gently removed her hand, which still held the offending member, the cause of all this commotion. Kara felt it was time to apologize and explain.

"I'm sorry I woke you, Cody," she said in a loud whisper. "I had hoped I wouldn't disturb anyone when I walked out."

Cody gave her a crooked grin. "I'm a light sleeper. It's your brother who appears he could sleep through anything. Don't worry about it. I noticed Pepper wasn't much help to you."

"I'm feeling really stupid though! I was looking forward to this campout, and it seems I've botched it. I'm not usually so clumsy."

Cody studied her for a moment before speaking. "Don't be so hard on yourself. I don't think the wound is all that bad. I do need to clean it up though. This is going to sting a little when I pour on the antiseptic."

Kara bit her lower lip as Cody applied the liquid, followed by ointment. Cody gently bandaged the foot like a pro, explaining that he had some medical training. He once served as a volunteer ambulance attendant a few years earlier. Noticing her scratched, soiled hands and the tear-streaked face, he retrieved warm water from a container suspended over the still-warm coals of the fire. Finding a washcloth, towel, and soap, he returned to Kara's side. She gratefully accepted the offered items and washed her face and hands. He then asked if there was anything else he could do for her, such as a drink of water or something. Not wanting to consider another trip to the bushes, she refused everything, suddenly feeling weary.

Walking on the heel of her injured foot, she was assisted to the tent entrance where she kindly thanked Cody and entered. Her foot and toe were beginning to throb as she crawled into the sleeping bag. It was some time before she was able to fall asleep. Her last thoughts were how comforting it felt to be carried in Cody's strong arms.

✢   ✢   ✢

The smell of fresh pancakes cooking and coffee brewing aroused Kara from her bed. She was suddenly very hungry. Hurriedly dressing into clean clothes, she came out of the tent to shyly approach the others. Four pair of eyes looked her direction, concern evident on their faces as they observed her bandaged foot and hobble. It was rather awkward to walk on the heel of her foot, but she managed.

"Good morning, Kara," Bobbie spoke brightly. "Cody explained to us about the accident and said it was no big deal. How is your foot?"

"It hurts a little, but I'm OK. I suppose you've noticed I'm not very agile," Kara said, attempting to make light of the incident. Davey noticed her embarrassment and offered her breakfast, which she gratefully accepted. Everyone talked of small events as they ate breakfast and then cleaned up.

Cody mentioned to Kara that the bandage should be changed. After close examination of the wound, he was pleased with what he saw. Carefully dressing the foot with a fresh bandage, he suggested she wear a sock. Davey promptly brought forth one of his socks that would be large enough to fit over the foot without too much discomfort.

Everyone agreed to ride and to let Hannah take the lead next. The Ralston family had camped often through the years, enabling them to discover some favorite haunts. One place in Hannah's mind was a cave set back in a nearby crop of rocks only a short distance away.

Davey assisted his sister in mounting Penny. It was easiest to pick her up bodily and place her on the animal. It hurt Kara's pride to have to be given special attention, but no one seemed to mind.

. . . All Things Become New . . .

Bobbie and Hannah doted over her now and then, and they all tried to get her involved in conversation from time to time.

It did not take the group long to reach the cave. Fortunately, it was molded into the side of the rock outcropping, so there was no steep or rocky path to walk. Kara was glad for Hannah's consideration. She was sure she would have made a greater fool of herself if she had had to walk uphill. Her foot still bothered her, and she was willing to sit on the horse and let the others explore. After some coaxing, she allowed Davey to lift her from the horse and help her to the cave entrance. Cody had already taken the liberty of checking out the interior for snakes or bears and declared it empty and safe to enter.

Cody was waiting with a flashlight at the entrance to escort them. He and Hannah had been in the cave numerous times to explore, but mostly it was a place to sit and chat like old friends. Hannah spoke in an animated tone about the adventures she and her brother had had in times past. A small pool of water lay in a bowl-shaped rock against one wall. A tiny trickle fed it from an unknown source in the depths of the cave. They all noticed the coolness of the cave and were excited about exploring it. After a fashion Kara discovered it was easier to walk on the side of her foot.

With a couple of flashlights, the group ventured further into the darkness of the cave. It was larger than they had expected. They entered another room far greater than the first, connected by a narrow passage, which they had followed. A shimmer of light shone from the ceiling, which was about ten feet high. Each of them offered their idea of what the cave had possibly been used for in the past. Cody mentioned that time was passing and if they wanted to get to the spot he had chosen for lunch, they had better be on their way.

Exiting the dimly lit cave to the sunshine outdoors temporarily blinded everyone. The sun felt good though after the coolness of the cave. Once their eyes had adjusted, they walked toward the horses, chatting as they went. Kara lost her balance with her awkward gait and would have fallen had Cody not been there to seize her arm before she fell. He did not let go until she was safely placed in the saddle. It was discouraging to be so awkward with the cumbersome foot. How did she ever manage to get herself into such a predicament? Cody was sensitive to Kara's discomfort and tried to make light of her situation, saying very little as he turned his attention to the others with conversation.

It was Cody's turn to lead the group. He promised them it was not far to their destination, but no one complained. Everyone seemed to enjoy the outing. It was about an hour later when they came to a mountain lake. It was so quiet and serene, that no one wanted to talk—just enjoy the silence. Now and then they heard a bird. Davey spotted a bald eagle in a dead tree perched near its nest in the branches. Suddenly, the majestic bird swooped down to skim the surface of the lake, flying away in one fluid motion with a fish in its sharp talons.

The day was proving to be rewarding and fun for all. Cody unsaddled and hobbled the horses to allow the animals to roam free and graze in the meadow while the group spent time at the lake. Hannah spread two blankets on the ground and unpacked the lunch Bobbie had prepared yesterday. Bobbie mentioned she had packed enough food to feed twice as many people and joked that they would have to camp out a couple of extra days to eat it all.

Lunch consisted of sandwiches, chips, and fresh fruit. Everyone had come prepared with bottled water. All the food tasted delicious in the fresh air. Cody and Davey had packed fishing poles. After lunch, they chose to try their hand at fishing while Hannah and Bobbie picked wildflowers. The plan was to catch fish for dinner.

Kara was content to sit on the blanket and observe the activity around her. Bobbie had packed a book in her supplies, which Kara was grateful for. It was too nice a day to be wasting it with a book though. Gingerly getting to her feet, she hobbled to where the guys were fishing, to converse with them. The trio made small talk. Cody told a few points of interest about the area and what it was like during different seasons of the year.

The rancher could not help but notice how the sun played on the blonde highlights of Kara's light brown hair. Her green eyes were clear and sparkling, brought on by the freshness of the day and activities. He was pleased to see she was enjoying herself, despite her bandaged foot.

It wasn't long before the men had caught more than enough trout for the meal. After expertly cleaning the fish and packing them in a soft cooler which they had filled with cold lake water, Cody and Hannah went to gather the horses and saddle them.

Mounted once again, the five rode for camp by a different route. Everyone appreciated being in the woods. Before they knew it, they were back to the campsite.

Cody had a fire going in no time. Hannah volunteered to cook the fish, pouring melted garlic butter over the fish and smothering them with chopped onions before wrapping them in aluminum foil. She then buried the fish, as well as the foil-wrapped potatoes, in the hot coals of the fire and allowed them time to cook.

Davey looked content as he sat on the ground with his back against a log, waiting for dinner. "Cody, my friend, I'm sure glad you thought of me when you decided to go on this excursion!"

Kara and Bobbie heartily joined in, expressing their delight with the campout.

Cody looked at his sister and smiled before directing his comment to his friends. "It really has been fun, hasn't it? Except for Kara's slight mishap, I suppose."

"I'm glad I was able to come, regardless," Kara said with a careless shrug of her shoulders.

Retrieving his Bible from his duffel bag, Davey thumbed through the pages of the Bible, suggesting now would be an appropriate time to read the Word since reading from the Scriptures was refreshing.

Kara was not certain as to where she fit in but was polite to listen to the reading of the Psalms. Hearing the Word read was like a soothing balm to her wounded heart. She was beginning to understand the love of God as she heard the Scriptures read. She had not thought about folks imposing their religion on her on this trip. It was probably because everyone accepted her, regardless of whether or not she went to church or Bible study. It was new to her to think of God as loving and tender. The Psalms spoke of the compassion and tender mercies of God. She had always thought of God as taking delight in seeing people brought to harm for their evil ways and sin. It was something to consider.

. . . Audrey Marr . . .

Following a delicious trout dinner and baked potatoes, everyone declared they had eaten too much and moaned a little. A walk would do them all good for sure. Kara chose to take it slow and easy, deciding that standing up and being in motion felt better than she had expected. Cody said he would walk with her to the nearby creek if she would like. Kara assured him she would.

Taking a seat on a large rock, the two began to converse. Hannah's rodeo competition was one of the subjects. It soon got more personal as Kara asked Cody the question, "Have you ever competed in rodeo, Cody?"

"Yes, I have. I've ridden bulls and broncs."

For some reason, his answer didn't surprise Kara. Her interest aroused, she questioned him further. "So, how did you do? Did you ever win anything?"

Cody gave her a crooked grin, one she was beginning to expect and to grow fond of.

"Yes, I did," Cody admitted. "I won a lot of times, making big money, as well as suffering a few broken bones along the way. It's a tough life in some ways. A lot of cowboys give their hundred percent in the arena and in partying. They work hard and drink and play hard too. I was one of those. I was raised in a Christian home, but I was sure I was missing out on something in life if I didn't go along with my peers. I got involved with the wrong crowd for some time. Getting drunk was a nightly occurrence.

"For some reason, my mom and dad kept loving me. Hannah tried hard to help me realize how much my actions hurt not only my family but myself too. She kept reminding me how much the Lord loved me and would never give up on me. I didn't care to hear what she had to say. I had set goals for myself and had my whole life ahead of me. Then one day while competing, riding a bull, I rode the animal to the bell and jumped off, twisting my ankle. The bull suddenly turned from the distractions of the rodeo clown, deciding he wasn't finished with me yet. If you have ever seen a one-ton bull eye to eye, you'd know what I mean!"

Kara's green eyes were huge, her face intently studying the man, wanting to hear the rest.

"I thought I was a goner, and in my fear I called out to God and told him I would quit my drinking and wild life-style if he would spare me. All of that seems suddenly unimportant when your life hangs in the balance. I knew I wasn't ready to die. I'd been to church most of my life and knew the consequences of a sinful life without God. I could almost feel the breath of that beast as he stood there in what was really only a matter of seconds. For no reason, the bull turned away to trot out the exit gate. It shook me up bad, but I was alive and was able to hobble from the arena instead of being carried off on a stretcher."

Cody sat musing silently for a few moments before speaking again. "I suddenly realized that even without having bargained with God, I didn't want to continue living the old life. I wanted something, or in this case, someone I could call on during the ups and downs of life."

Kara was not sure how to respond to the story. She could see for herself that this man sitting beside her was not wild and certainly not a drunk. "I'm glad for you, Cody. I can see one couldn't have a more loving family than yours."

Turning to look directly into her face, he said with conviction, "No matter our past or life-style, Kara, the Lord is for everyone. He loves you as much as He does me. There's no difference in His eyes. It's not how badly we live, or the good or bad things we do in our lives. The Bible says we are all sinners." Desiring to clarify his statement, he pulled out a pocket-sized New Testament from the rear pocket of his jeans, leafing through the Scriptures to find what he wanted to read. "Here it says in Romans 3:22–24: 'This righteousness from God comes through faith in Jesus Christ to all who believe. There is no difference, for all have sinned and fall short of the glory of God, and are justified freely by His grace, through redemption that came by Jesus Christ.'"

Cody closed the Testament and looked to Kara again. "Redemption means to buy back or to pay a debt. Jesus Christ bought you and me—everyone. He paid the price for our sins. It's for us to choose to accept the gift He gave—His life—that we might have life eternal."

It was all hitting too close to home for Kara, and she began to feel uncomfortable. She politely smiled and said nothing as he turned his attention to the creek flowing close-by. He desired to give her a chance to absorb all that he had said.

She could see Cody's relationship was as real for him as it was for the others, including her brother. She squirmed some, suddenly uneasy with the turn of the conversation to her. It was as though an invisible, gentle hand had reached down to caress her, tugging at her heartstrings. She was glad to be interrupted by the other three approaching.

"This weather is absolutely gorgeous, isn't it, Kara?" Bobbie asked, Hannah alongside.

"It sure is. What do you have there in your hand?"

"Oh, Hannah and I picked these while we took our walk. Aren't they lovely?"

"They really are!"

Hannah sat down beside Kara to allow a better view of the bouquet she had taken from Bobbie. "Here's the yellow wild sunflower, the red Indian paintbrush, the purple coneflower, the lupine that blooms in various colors of white, blue, and purple, and the pink bitterroot, which is the state flower. It seems that as one species of flower is finished blooming for the season, another variety can be found. Mountain wildflowers are in bloom all the time during the summer months."

Bobbie was excited with the bouquet of flowers. "Wow! I think I'll try to press some of these flowers to use to decorate stationery paper. I could use clear contact paper or such to do it. I'm glad I packed some waxed paper." She hurried away to the packed supplies to follow through with her plans.

Davey came alongside the group and suggested they return to camp and make dessert.

Cody smiled, helping Kara to her feet as he spoke. "I never turn down dessert, myself!"

Everyone walked back to camp, chatting along the way.

"So, do you have a deliciously fattening after-dinner delight in mind for us, Bobbie?" Hannah asked as they approached camp.

"Yes, I do," Bobbie stated. Her eyes twinkling, she smiled at Kara. "I had YOU in mind, Kara, when I decided on this one."

Pulling out a bag of marshmallows, several solid chocolate candy bars, and a box of graham crackers, Bobbie walked over to the campfire. Pleased to note the bed of hot coals, Bobbie said,

"Everyone needs to roast a few marshmallows on a stick so we can have s'mores."

"Mmmm. That sounds wonderful, Bobbie," Kara said, her eyes sparkling with delight. "Chocolate and marshmallows should be a winning combination! I'm not sure how you make them without the convenience of a microwave."

"It's really quite simple," Bobbie informed her. Once her marshmallows were lightly browned, she continued, "You take the marshmallows like so." Placing a graham cracker above and below the marshmallow, she expertly slid the marshmallow off the stick. Bobbie then proceeded to unwrap a candy bar, break off a piece, and place it between the graham cracker and marshmallow. "The chocolate doesn't melt much this way, but it sure tastes good!"

She took a bite, rolling her eyes with pleasure to complete the demonstration.

Everyone laughed at her actions, quickly assembling their own s'mores bar, so they could enjoy it as well, even if it was a bit messy.

They followed dessert with a sing-a-long around the campfire as darkness settled over the happy campers. Hannah thought it would be a good time to share a memory. "My beloved brother and I were told to clean out behind the horses one wintry day. I think I was about fourteen years old, so that would make him seventeen."

Cody shook his head in disbelief and pulled his cowboy hat over his eyes.

Hannah continued, "It's not the most pleasant job and neither of us wanted to be there. It was more fun to be riding horses, to check cattle or doing just about anything else than pitching horse manure with a pitchfork. Our tempers were short as we yelled back and forth, arguing with one another as we pitched dung into the wheelbarrow. It was my turn to wheel the manure to the place out back of the barn. Unfortunately, with all of our arguing, we had heaped the dung high. It was more than I could really handle, but Cody refused to help me. Disgusted with him and figuring I could do it myself regardless, I gave the wheelbarrow a push. I didn't get far out the barn door when the wheelbarrow tipped over. I was so mad at Cody I started picking up frozen horse dung and throwing it at him like rocks. He yelled and told me to quit, but I was too angry to stop." Hannah started to chuckle.

By now, Cody was sitting upright. He pointed an accusing finger at his sister as he interrupted her to give his explanation of the way it had been. "Yeah, and she knew I had suffered many times for hitting her. Dad and Mom made it clear that a man did not hit a young woman, even if she was in the form of a tormenting sister! The only thing I knew to do was to grab hold of her until she calmed down, since she blocked my way of escape. Man, I thought I had hold of a wild cat for sure when I got my arms around her!" Cody shook his head with the memory. "I still can't believe I lived to tell the story. I had bruised shins for weeks afterward. It wasn't long before I decided it was easier to empty the wheelbarrow myself than to deal with her. I told her I'd clean out the barn myself and to leave me alone."

The others had a good laugh as Hannah tore a wad of grass from beside her and threw it at her brother.

"OK, Kara, it's your turn. What awful antic has your brother done to you in the past?" Bobbie questioned.

Kara had an impish gleam to her eye as she lightly tapped her chin with an index finger. "Well, let me see . . . I do remember the time Davey was good and mad at me for getting into his prized model cars. I was probably ten years old. He had worked hard piecing them together, getting them painted and such. I took it upon myself to help him finish one particular model. I proceeded to paint and make a royal mess, spilling some of the paint, too. Fortunately, there was newspaper underneath the paint jar. Painting didn't seem all that much fun to me, so I decided to leave, mess and all."

Kara rolled her eyes as she recalled her brother's reaction to finding his tidy work area a disaster. "I'm so glad we get along as well as we do now! Boy, was he ever mad at me! Mom and Dad weren't at home, so there was no one to run to for help. I decided to hide in my bedroom closet, hoping he wouldn't find me, but he did. Somehow, I managed to get past him and was able to lock myself in the bathroom until our parents got home. When they found out what I had done, they made me take my allowance money and buy Davey another bottle of paint and a model car. That was worse than a spanking! I had been saving a long time for a bike I wanted and could only have one if I bought it with my own money. I suppose Mom and Dad believed I would appreciate the bike more by buying it myself. I still remember that smug look you wore, Davey, as I handed the money over the counter to the store clerk to purchase the model and paint you had chosen."

Davey did not look regretful at all as he spoke. "Sorry, Kar. That model you ruined was to be entered in the county fair in a few days. I had to work extra hard to get another one ready." Smiling, he added, "I bet you learned a lesson though, didn't you?"

"You don't have to rub it in, brother! I was set back several weeks after that, but, yes, I did learn my lesson on that deal."

"Your turn, Bobbie," Hannah informed her. "Do you have any brothers or sisters?"

"No, I don't. Listening to the four of you makes me a bit envious. Growing up an only child can be lonely at times." She felt somewhat melancholy, just thinking about it.

Hannah thought it wise to change the subject to other childhood memories that Bobbie could relate to. The group learned a lot about one another that evening, laughing until their sides hurt, making it difficult to catch one's breath.

It was a pleasant finale to the evening. Everyone was reluctant to see it end.

Bobbie and Hannah made Kara promise to wake one or the other of them should she need to go out during the night. Kara did not want to impose, but after receiving some stern looks from the two, she agreed. It was wonderful having such friends, she thought, as she crawled inside her sleeping bag and went to sleep.

✢   ✢   ✢

Everyone woke Sunday morning feeling refreshed, considering they had gotten to bed late. Not wanting to waste the day in bed, they were up and moving by 7 A.M. Even Kara was anxious to greet the new day, regardless of the fact that she had been up three times in the night.

Many species of birds chirped in the trees surrounding the campsite. Cody pointed out to the company the blue Stellers Jay and gray Camp Robber among the more common birds, such as sparrows and chickadees.

Breakfast was blueberry pancakes, eggs, and sausage. Davey joked about how rough camping could be.

Cody offered to change Kara's bandage and examine her foot. Though still tender, the wound was healing nicely. "It looks good, Kara. Some say the mountain air causes wounds to heal quicker and people to stay healthier."

Kara smiled at the remark. "I agree with you, Cody. The air in Montana is definitely better than the air in most cities I've visited back east. Have you ever been west of the Mississippi?"

"No, I never have. I always thought it would be nice to travel back that way in the fall to see the changing color of the leaves that I've seen in magazines."

"Fall is a beautiful time of year. Maybe you will some day."

Cody suggested they have a morning devotion together and then go exploring. He read Psalm 103 in his pleasant baritone voice with strength, conviction, and expression. Kara heard the words clearly about the compassion and love of God. The Scriptures confirmed to the young widow what she had been hearing often since coming to Montana: "He does not treat us as our sins deserve or repay us according to our iniquities. For as high as the heavens are above the earth, so great is his love for those who fear him . . ."

For the first time, Kara allowed herself to honestly consider the truth of the words read and to take them to heart, to think and see herself as a person who had been rejecting God all her life. She recognized that He exists and He sees and knows everything. God was beginning to look different in her mind's eye, more than she had thought possible. He was becoming real to her in a way she had never considered before, as someone personal who was tender, loving, and caring—much like her dad and Jonny had been to her. Much like her brother. This fresh revelation she had was overwhelming and scary. It was as though a light had been turned on to illuminate a refreshing and new understanding of who God was and how frail and minute she was.

Kara thought these ideas were happening too fast to suit her. She needed time alone to digest this new knowledge. If it were possible, she would have run away somewhere to be alone, but there was no way to do that without drawing attention to herself. She could not fault her brother and friends, because she did realize their actions were out of love for her. Kara guessed she would have to make the best of the situation and pretend nothing was different. A part of her was fearful and another part wanted to weep. It was difficult to hold back the tears in her confusion.

She was thankful that Cody chose that moment to pray. Kara could not remember what was said. She kept her head bowed and eyes closed in an attempt to bring her emotions under control. Suddenly, Hannah and Bobbie moved closer to press against her on either side, each putting an arm around her following an "Amen" from Cody, ending his prayer.

"Kara, I think you're beginning to realize the love God has for you, aren't you?" Bobbie asked, her voice quiet and soft.

Lest she betray her feelings, Kara could only nod her head up and down. She felt as though God Himself was wrapping His arms around her in the form of her two friends. She kept her head down, eyes averted, certain that if she looked at her friend, she would burst into tears. Had she looked, Kara would have seen Bobbie's eyes brimming with tears, her heart tender toward Kara.

"Would you like to pray with me, or could I explain anything more to you?"

Kara shook her head. She decided she needed more time to think and consider it all.

"Feel free to come talk to me any time, day or night, OK?"

Feeling she had gotten hold of her emotions, Kara looked up and told her friend she would. She sensed everyone's eyes upon her now and wished it was not so. She squirmed, uncomfortable with the thought that she always seemed to be the center of attention for one reason or another.

Davey stood, offering to help Cody saddle the horses so they could get under way. He gave his sister an affectionate hug before walking away. How he ached for her! He knew the decision was one only she could make. If she would only stop struggling with the Lord and realize He wanted only good for her!

After the horses were saddled and everyone mounted, Hannah took the lead in the direction opposite the one they had taken the day before. Following a much-used game trail, the party rode for a while in single file through the woods with no particular destination in mind. The smell of the pine trees was appealing, as well as the sounds of birds and squirrels in the woods. Often, the only sounds were the creaking of saddles and the breathing of horses.

At one point, the riders dismounted to stretch their muscles and walk, enjoying the exercise. Kara spent most of her time in the saddle. Shortly after they had mounted their horses again, they discovered a herd of mule deer. Hannah counted twenty in all. Many had young at their sides. They looked almost comical with their large ears, which were the first thing one noticed.

Further on, as they were riding back toward camp for lunch, Cody sighted a black bear sow with two cubs. Making certain the dog was closeby, he suggested they give her plenty of space. Seeing the animals in their natural environment thrilled the riders. It was proving to be an adventurous and rewarding morning.

Camp was not as they had left it. It had been ransacked. Cody cautioned the group to take it slow. He imagined the culprit was a bear. They had been careful about storing food so as not to attract wild animals, but evidently they had not been careful enough. The tents were flattened and the camp was in total disarray. The picnic coolers had been opened and the contents spilled on the ground. Pancake flour and plastic bags containing food were scattered on the ground. The culprit had eaten well. Hannah noticed animal tracks and showed them to Cody, who confirmed the intruder was a grizzly bear. They were relieved the animal was gone. No one wanted to tangle with a grizzly!

It took a while for them to clean up the mess. Fortunately, the tents were in fine shape. They salvaged a sparse amount of food that had somehow escaped the bear's healthy appetite. It was obvious there was not enough to satisfy the appetite of five people. Cody suggested they make the best of the situation and go fishing. Fish sounded good to everyone. Snacking on granola bars missed by the bear, the campers mounted their horses for the ride to the lake, determined that no bear was going to spoil their outing.

An hour later, they arrived at the lake with its placid, clear waters. Everyone helped unsaddle and hobble the horses, so they would be free to graze. Dave noticed the eagle in the same tree snag. The beauty and quietness was a soothing balm.

With only two fishing poles, the men traded off now and then to allow the women a chance to fish. Bobbie caught a nice trout. Hannah was an old hand at fishing. She caught three fish in no time. Kara had fished, mostly for pan fish or Walleye, back east. Fishing for trout was a new challenge to her, but she was willing to give it a try. She got some nibbles but no bites. Eventually, Cody informed the group that they had plenty of fish. His parents had promised to have a barbecue for everyone upon their return from camping, so he was certain they would not starve that day.

Davey started a fire near the lakeshore, and the fish, wrapped in foil, were cooked in the coals. Everyone declared the trout delicious. Eating outdoors in the fresh air and sunshine tended to have that effect. Laughter and talk were hearty. The lunch could not have been better had they been dining in a restaurant with fine china and elegant décor. What better way to be eating than in the wilderness among God's creation, the tall pine trees serving as a roof above, a fallen log for a chair, and friends all around?

There was not much clean up needed following the simple meal. Cody said that time was getting away, so they'd best get organized and ride for the campsite, where there was still packing to do for the trip down the mountain. The horses were caught and saddled quickly. Kara was now able to mount her horse with no assistance, so long as she placed her foot carefully.

Returning to the ravaged camp, everyone worked efficiently to tidy the area and leave little trace that anyone had been there. No one cared to disturb the beauty of the place any more than was necessary, desiring to leave it in its natural state for someone else to enjoy.

The riders mounted and took their leave. They each looked back as they rode away, at the place that had been so much fun and fellowship. They hated to see it all end, but they knew that in the days ahead their thoughts would return to the memories they had made that special weekend.

✣   ✣   ✣

Soon they were back at the ranch and unloading gear. Rita and Martin Ralston were happy to see everyone. It was obvious they had all had a good time, regardless of Kara's mishap or the bear. An excited Hannah ushered Bobbie and Kara into the house while the two men cared for the horses. She was anxious to share with her parents all they had experienced. The Ralstons were just as eager to hear. While the steaks were cooking on the grill, the group lounged in the spacious living room.

Cody and Davey entered the house to the smell of grilled steak, the aroma causing everyone's mouth to water in anticipation of a delicious meal. Martin was the official cook at the grill. He delivered the meat and some shish kabobs to the dining room to be served with rice and fresh fruit salad.

Rita seated everyone as she saw fit, trying not to be obvious in the arrangement. She made certain that Dave was between Bobbie and Cody and that Kara and Hannah were on the opposite side, while she and Martin sat at either end of the large table. After Martin blessed the food, they gladly filled their plates. Conversation was light and the food hearty. Dessert was next. Rita had made a fresh apple pie to be served with ice cream. Though everyone was already feeling full, they could hardly refuse it. A contented lot they were. The meal was a fitting end to a wonderful weekend.

Rita had plenty of help in the kitchen following the meal. Clean up was accomplished in record time. The hostess was appreciative of anything that was done for her. No one minded in the least, especially after such a sumptuous feast.

Since they had nearly an hour's drive ahead of them, Davey suggested they leave about 8 P.M. After expressing thanks to the Ralston family, the trio left the ranch. A contented number of people retired that night, remembering what it was like to be in the mountains, snuggled in their sleeping bags and grateful for the experience in the woods.

... 17

Before long, Kara was enjoying summer in Montana. She kept busy working at the auto body shop, cleaning, cooking, and gardening. Her injured foot had healed quickly following the camping trip.

Kara also spent plenty of time with Emily Rose, who was growing quickly. She was the picture of health with her round, rosy cheeks, chubby hands and legs, and the beautiful, dark, long lashes she had inherited from her mother. Emily was truly a real person in her own right. Sandy stated that Daddy was already wrapped around Emily's tiny finger. The happy baby was a joy to the couple.

Sandy and Drew were both excited for Kara concerning the coming baby. Drew had been casually acquainted with Jonny before moving to Montana and had found Jonny friendly and likeable. Sandy and Kara spent a lot of time discussing the baby, realizing it truly was a special event in the lives of everyone involved.

Kara was in maternity clothes now, her body showing a gentle roundness with the growing baby. The first time she felt the fluttery movement of the little one within her, she was indescribably excited. It made the pregnancy seem real, not a figment of her imagination. Being able to hold and cuddle Emily was rewarding for the young mother-to-be. It made her eager to hold her own little one. Thinking of the months that stretched before her until she could cuddle her baby seemed an eternity, causing her to chafe and wish for the time to fly. December seemed a long way off. It would not bother her should the baby choose to be born sooner. She was feeling good and enjoying the pregnancy, so she told herself she should be content with the waiting.

Bobbie often spent time with Davey and Kara. It was obvious to all who knew Dave and Bobbie that there was interest beyond friendship between the couple. Kara was sincerely hoping the two would make a match of it. She dearly loved Bobbie and could not think of a better person for her brother to spend the rest of his life with.

Following the camping trip, Kara had taken interest in the Wednesday evening Bible study. Although hesitant to attend church, the young woman found the Bible study, consisting of a small group of people, less intimidating. She was now familiar with the songs sung during the worship time, having heard them often around campfires. Dennis Cooper had a way of teaching the Bible that was simple enough for a child to understand, yet thought-provoking to an adult. It was the love of those around her that had convinced her to attend the Bible study. She came to know everyone well and was always eager to see Hannah and Cody and to know how their week had gone, when ranching or rodeos weren't keeping them too busy.

Often when Kara found herself alone in her brother's house, she sat by her bedroom window reading Davey's Bible. At times the words made sense, but most of the time she was confused. The book of Psalms was her favorite.

One particular afternoon, she longed for her own Bible and decided to ask Davey what Bible version would be best for her. Struck by a sudden thought, she rose from her window chair and hurried to the large, wooden trunk at the foot of her bed. Carefully kneeling in her slightly awkward condition, she lifted the lid of the trunk to root among the contents. Finding what she was looking for at the very bottom, she sat on the floor, holding the cherished item. A few tears escaped her closed eyelids as she remembered. Opening her eyes, she looked at the book as she placed it on her lap, running her hands over the smooth leather with tenderness,

. . . All Things Become New . . .

almost reverently. Turing the crisp pages of the Bible, the young widow came to the familiar script, written by her brother's hand. Davey had presented the Bible to her late husband only a week or so before Jonny had died. The pain was not as sharp as it had been, but it still hurt knowing she would never see her Jonny again.

She recalled how annoyed she had been with Jonny that he could get so excited about a Bible, as he grinned from ear to ear at the gift. Davey had seemed pleased with his brother-in-law's reaction and offered to show Jonny scriptures they had been discussing. The two men had immediately taken a seat on the living room sofa to read and share. With chagrin, Kara had made the excuse of getting dinner started and left the two. So engrossed in the Bible, they had not seemed to hear her excuse.

Kara now felt shame for her reaction. How could she have been so cold? How many times, up until the day Jonny died, had she seen him reading this very Bible and mocked him for it? His reaction was only love, acting as though he had not noticed the caustic comments she made in her bitterness. This irritated her more than if he had responded in anger. The new Jonny was not perfect, but he was much changed since the time when he might have retaliated.

Sitting beside the trunk, Jonny's Bible in her lap, Kara sighed, feeling a spiritual heaviness in her chest. At times she felt she carried the weight of the world. She was aware of the fact that she was lacking somehow. Then the Scriptures she had heard at Bible study came to mind. Curious, she returned to her window seat and opened the Bible to chapter one of the book of John. Dennis had begun teaching from the book of John last week. Having never read the Bible, she had been at a loss in the discussion. She was confident it would help her immensely to read ahead in preparation for next week's study. Where better to begin than the first chapter?

Her excitement mounted as she read Jonny's Bible, a link with the past and what would prove to be a healing balm to her wounded heart.

Engrossed, Kara lost track of time. Jesus was someone she desired to know. Reading about Him, she wished she could have lived in Bible times and experienced knowing the Man in person. She glanced at the clock and was startled to see the time. Davey would be home soon and she had not even begun dinner preparations! Carefully placing the Bible on her nightstand, she left for the kitchen.

✥   ✥   ✥

One Friday evening, Cody called the office to invite Davey and Kara out for dinner. Davey had done a first rate job repainting Cody's personal truck and had been more than fair with the charges. Cody wished to show his gratitude by treating the two. Kara did not think she, as the secretary, should be part of the offer, but Cody assured her it would be fine or he would not have asked. Life had been hectic at the ranch, and he was looking forward to a break from the fast pace. He had not had much fellowship and was eager to visit with them. Everyone agreed to Saturday evening, and Cody offered to pick up his guests at 5 P.M.

When it came to hospitality, Cody was as gracious as his parents were. The rancher looked ruggedly handsome in his western-style jacket, white shirt and bolo, black jeans, and polished boots. He had chosen a fine Italian restaurant. Both Kara and Davey were hungry for a true Italian dish of lasagna. Cody ordered a manicotti dish. The server presented breadsticks, and the three conversed easily as they snacked on the bread and waited for their orders. The trio then enjoyed their steaming entrees, the pleasant atmosphere and one another's company.

There was a lot of catching up to do. Kara asked about Hannah, who was competing in a rodeo in central Montana and aspiring to make it to the nationals.

"There's a rodeo in two weeks in a town northeast of here," Cody explained, "about an hour and a half away. Hannah is competing there. Would the two of you be interested in going? That's providing, of course, the heat doesn't bother you too much, Kara."

Kara's green eyes sparkled as she turned to question her brother.

Davey did not hesitate to answer with a nod. He had been to a number of rodeos since living in Montana and wanted his sister to see one.

Kara assured Cody she would be fine. She enjoyed the dry western air and did not miss the humidity that was so prevalent in the east.

... All Things Become New ...

Satisfied with their response, Cody noticed how Kara continued to glow with the pregnancy. It appeared to agree with her. Because of the warmth of the day, she had styled her hair in a cool, casual fashion that he found becoming. The simple but attractive floral, mint-green dress made her green eyes even more captivating.

He wondered, as he often did, what it would be like to be married to a woman like her. He admired her a great deal. The young widow was stronger than she would ever give herself credit for. He was pleased to know she was attending the Bible study regularly with her brother. The rancher made subtle inquiries into her well-being if he happened to miss a meeting himself. Bobbie was a good source and seemed caring and sensitive about his concerns for Kara. He prayed daily for Kara's salvation. In some ways, he was glad she was not one to make quick decisions and jump in hastily with both feet.

Cody prayed that the seed sowed would land in good soil, that it would root deeply and produce a crop for the Lord. He prayed the woman would become solid and grounded in the Lord, as well. His desire was that when she came to the Lord, it would be with all her being. He had observed at the Bible study that she was very receptive. Possibly the camping trip had been a turning point of some kind for her. He was willing to be patient; he could wait.

It bothered Cody to consider Kara returning to stay in the east. His first thought was that he would go after her. But then, that was hasty; he didn't know how she felt about him. She might not have any interest in him whatsoever, especially since the wedding band was still on her finger, ever reminding him of where her heart still lay. He was shocked to realize that his feelings for Kara ran deeper than he had been willing to admit.

None of this showed on his face as conversation flowed between brother and sister. Cody was brought out of his deliberation, leaving him troubled as Dave directed a question to him. Cody answered as best he could, took a deep breath, and pretended he was still enjoying himself. The fact was, he suddenly wished for the evening to end so he could be alone for a while, even though he took pleasure in their company. He needed time to think, to consider where all these newly discovered emotions were leading him.

After dinner, Cody took his guests home. Dave invited him in for a video and popcorn. The rancher declined, making what he felt was a lame excuse, but the best he could come up with.

... 18

Cody typically visited a particular spot on the ranch when he needed a retreat, like tonight. He took an easy drive on a long, winding road that led to a pond which was spring fed, overflowing at one end to drain into a creek that ran through the ranch. Even in the driest of weather, this pond was always full. A variety of wildlife swam in the water. Presently he spotted a pair of ducks.

Were ducks committed for life to one another, never taking another mate? He pondered the idea, feeling discouraged to think he hardly knew Kara and to note the strong possibility of losing her. Standing at the water's edge, the young rancher chose a flat stone from the ground and tossed it in the water, skipping it along the pond surface.

Why did things have to be so complicated, much like the ripples he had created with the stone he had thrown? How much did he want her to belong to him? How long was he willing to wait? Since she was young, she might desire to marry again, given time and the right circumstances. This Jonny Madison was a hard act to follow. Dave had nothing but good to say about his late brother-in-law. It sounded as though he had been genuine in his relationship and love for his wife, which is the way it should be.

. . . All Things Become New . . .

    Cody's life-style was quite different from those of people back east, he was sure. Yet Kara seemed to have adapted to Montana; she appeared to be enjoying herself and the time spent with her brother.
    Why was he so drawn to the young widow? Was it because of the circumstances that had brought her to Montana? He did not think so. Maybe it was because she was the kind of person he had always desired to marry. She had many qualities, including beauty, but beauty could be a deceiving trait; it was not at the top of his list. He more highly valued her other traits.
    Before his salvation, Cody had dated a woman whose beauty caused male heads to turn, their mouths gaping like fools as they stared at her. Unfortunately, that woman had known it and played on others' affections. She had made Cody nothing but miserable!
    Materially, this woman always wanted nothing but the best. She sulked and pouted if she didn't often get nice things to brag about to her friends. Quickly Cody could see she was a woman with expensive tastes who would never be satisfied, always desiring fancy, expensive restaurants and such. Realizing he was just another possession to dangle on a string and jerk around like a wooden puppet to suit her fancy, Cody had nipped the relationship in the bud. He thanked God many times for having His hand on him even when he was not aware of it. He was sure the prayers of his parents had played a large part in it all. No, outward beauty was not important to Cody.
    What he desired was a woman who would share his faith, a woman who loved the Lord and was dedicated to live holy and walk righteous before Him. Taking the pocket-sized New Testament and Psalms he carried with him—his constant companion—he turned to the Psalms to seek solace. Sunset was not until 11 P.M., so there was still plenty of daylight to read by. Sitting on a large flat rock nearby, he knew this was bigger than he had the wisdom to handle, but he also knew Someone who knew his deepest yearnings and thoughts and who had all wisdom.
    He reverently bowed his head to pray. "Lord, You know me better than I know myself. All of this is beyond me. I'm feeling so overwhelmed. You know I desire someone who would be my best friend, as well as my mate, but You also know that, more importantly, I desire a godly wife, so that together we can serve You. All I

know to do is to commit all my cares to You. Not my will, but Yours be done.

"I pray for Kara's sake that she would surrender her life to You, that she would find the inner peace she needs. Please take care of the little one she's carrying. I'm sure she's grateful to be having the baby with her husband gone. Help Dave and Bobbie to minister Your truth to her, and help her to receive it. Thank You for bringing her west, if for no other reason than to heal her hurt and bring her to salvation in You.

"I need Your discernment to know what my true feelings are. If Kara is not for me, then I pray You will make that clear so I will know and accept it. You know sometimes, Lord, that I could use a rap alongside my head. But I thank You for Your patience, mercy, and grace toward me. I thank You for dealing with me in love only. Thank You, Jesus, for what You did for me on the cross. I pray that Kara would realize that same truth for herself. Bless my friends, Dave and Bobbie, and the time they spend together, getting to know one another. May they know Your will too. I ask and pray all these things in the precious name of Jesus. Amen."

Following the prayer, Cody sat quietly to absorb the stillness around him and to think about the Lord's goodness. He knew he had to leave all his cares in God's hands and to trust that if Kara were not for him, then the Lord would bring him someone who was. Sometimes he felt the hand of time was passing too quickly. He would soon be twenty-six years old, yet he knew time meant nothing to God. Patience was not one of his better virtues, but he would try, with God's help. He would have to continue to take things slowly and keep his emotions in check—or attempt to anyway.

✤   ✤   ✤

Kara was not aware of the misery her friend Cody was experiencing where she was concerned. Her days continued to be busy. She was happy for her brother and Drew that business was going well. Integrity and honesty played a large part in their success. Their reputation proceeded them as honest business partners who were also reasonable in fees.

Kara was grateful for the air-conditioned office. It was a warm summer, making it difficult to have an appetite. She never understood how Davey could continue to have such a hearty appetite—rain, snow, sun, or shine. She would admit though, she did have cravings and hunger in the night when she should be sleeping.

The garden Kara and Davey had planted produced more than they could use. She took the liberty to freeze some of the vegetables. Occasionally, she gave fresh vegetables to Sandy and Bobbie. Both were busy gals who always appreciated the vegetables. Kara often served stir-fry dinners, but Davey never complained. He said Kara's cuisine beat anything he could cook.

The day of the rodeo dawned warm and sunny. Davey quit work early to give them plenty of time for fun. He and Kara met Cody at his ranch, as it was en route. It was a small town event, but it always had a big turnout, as everyone around for miles sought a break from work and a chance to meet with friends. Folks from that area would use any excuse to get together.

Kara arranged her hair, which the sun had bleached a lighter brown with blonde highlights, into a French braid. Looking through her wardrobe, she wondered, *What does one wear to a rodeo?* She chose shorts and a sleeveless, light blue maternity blouse. It already felt hot and it wasn't noon yet. Tennis shoes seemed in order for the day.

Downstairs in the kitchen, she packed plenty of cold drinks in a cooler, as well as sandwiches and fresh fruit. Davey appeared in the doorway to say he was ready. Kara opened doors for him as he carried the awkward cooler to the Blazer.

When the two got to the ranch, they were surprised to see Bobbie. She had caught wind of their excursion and had taken Hannah's invitation to watch the barrel racer perform. Davey was pleased to see her and offered to drive everyone to the rodeo.

The men took the front seats and the women settled in the back. Even though the women had seen each other only yesterday, they were excited and had much to talk about. Before the four of them realized it, they arrived at the rodeo. Quite a crowd had already gathered. People came early for an event such as this. The contestants were always early to exercise their horses before competition, much like athletes prepare. These cowboys and cowgirls were truly athletes in a class by themselves. Observing the riders in the arena, Kara turned to Cody, "I don't see Hannah among those in the arena. Where could she be?"

Cody smiled. "Hannah is probably in the area to our right where you see all the trucks and trailers that the contestants drove here. She prefers to be off by herself when she warms up her horse. She says it's relaxing. It gives her time alone to focus on the competition."

Noticing Kara's disappointment, he added, "Don't worry. Hannah promised to look us up after the barrel racing, which is what she's competing in. It won't be a long wait since they will have the women compete first."

"Don't mind me, Cody," Kara said with a sigh. "I guess I'm excited about being here."

Cody put her at ease with a reassuring smile.

The women taking the lead, the four moved toward the grandstand. People milled around as everyone waited for the rodeo to begin. Kara was pleased to note the roof above the seating area. It was hot just the same. She was glad she had brought her sunglasses and hat to ward off some of the heat and glare of the sun. Cody chose the seating. As they stood waiting for the competition to start, Cody pointed out Hannah, who was riding her mount in a slow canter outside the arena.

Hannah made an attractive picture in her dark blue western outfit with matching hat. Her horse wore a matching blue saddle blanket, as well as leg wrappings. Silver on the saddle, breast collar, and bridle glistened in the sun. Kara knew the horse's name was Levi. The mouse-colored gelding knew his business. Hannah had trained him well. He looked powerful, yet beautiful, as he moved through the paces Hannah asked of him.

One could not help but notice that all the competitors were expert horsemen. Kara felt like a novice as she watched them exercising their mounts much like Hannah was doing.

The rodeo announcer spoke into the microphone to introduce the two women on horseback who entered the empty arena, one bearing the American flag and the other, the Montana state flag. They rode around the arena making a complete circle, then turned toward the center and stopped their mounts, facing the crowd in the grandstand as an attractive woman approached the announcer's microphone to sing the national anthem. All stood and removed hats for the song. Following the anthem, everyone clapped and cheered as the riders exited the arena.

Three volunteer cowboys rolled barrels to specific areas marked in the dirt inside the arena to form a triangle pattern. The barrel racers would ride in a cloverleaf pattern around the barrels. First up was the youngest contestant to compete that day. Only thirteen years old, the girl had no fear as she charged toward the barrel on her right at a speed most would not dare. She circled that barrel, then rode toward the left barrel—the one directly in front of her after she had circled the first barrel. Then she rode toward the middle barrel—the farthest one away. Circling it, the girl pressed her mount to greater speed toward the finish line, sliding to a stop before running into the fence. The electronic timer recorded her time. She did not seem pleased with the numbers and exited the arena to the sound of the applause. No sooner had she left the arena when Kara could see another barrel racer ready to enter the arena and understood the riders wanted to be running their horses at the start of the timer.

"I can't imagine riding a horse at such breakneck speed and still having control of the horse!" Kara mentioned to Cody, breathless with excitement. "It's obvious the horses are well trained and enjoy running like that. I have nothing but respect for all of them and if it were up to me, I'd give them all a blue ribbon."

Cody laughed. "But there wouldn't be any point in having a rodeo if everyone got a blue ribbon. The riders wouldn't work as hard as they do to get first place—and we would be bored."

"Just the same," Kara stated matter-of-factly, "I wouldn't want to be the judge!"

Kara didn't realize that her hands were in her lap, tight-fisted and sweaty, as one rider after another entered and exited the arena. Now and then she firmly grasped the arm of Bobbie or Cody, who were sitting on either side of her.

Bobbie thoroughly enjoyed herself too. Occasionally, she leapt from her seat to shout, "Go, go, go!" She rooted for everyone.

Dave was surprised to note the volume of Bobbie's shouts, smiling and shaking his head in amused disbelief. A few times, Dave received the brunt of Bobbie's fingernails in his flesh as she got caught up in the action. Neither he nor Cody minded their plight, delighted that the women were enjoying themselves. Occasionally, Kara and Bobbie realized what they were doing and apologized to their victims.

At one point, Davey leaned back, got Cody's attention and shouted above the noise of the crowd, "We should do this more often! I didn't expect these ladies to show such enthusiasm for the sport!"

Cody grinned, nodding his head in agreement.

When Hannah's turn came, Kara was ready to explode with excitement for her friend. Hannah charged past the starting line, her long, blonde braid flying behind her as she circled the barrels. Levi ran at breakneck speed for the finish line and slid to a stop once past the imaginary line. Her time was announced and loud cheers erupted for the attractive rider. It appeared Hannah was in the running, presently taking third place. Hundredths of a second would determine the final outcome. It was always a guessing game and one never knew. The saying, "It's not over 'til it's over," was especially true in this sport.

Some competitors were eliminated and the semi-finalists were announced. Hannah was among the semi-finalists. After another ride, she moved up to second place. Kara noted the stiff competition and was glad she did not have to ride around the barrels. She could not help but smirk at the thought. She, with her growing stomach, riding a horse at breakneck speed! She'd have a good excuse for not competing. There was no way she would endanger this little one. Following this tender thought, her baby rewarded her with a gentle reminder.

Cody wondered at Kara's smile. He was not sure it was his place to ask, but Kara's facial expressions were so endearing.

Amid the noise of the crowd, the rancher leaned toward the mother-to-be. "What do you find so amusing?"

She cocked her head to the side and smiled at him. "I was thinking how silly I'd look out there in my condition, riding a horse like these barrel racers."

Cody rolled his eyes and laughed with her. "I don't think so, Kara!"

... All Things Become New ...

With a short break before the finals, the four had some refreshments in an attempt to cool off.

Bobbie took a long drink of cold, bottled juice. "Mmmm! This is wonderful! I didn't know a cold drink could taste so good!" Glancing toward Dave, she added with a mischievous gleam in her eye, "I guess I worked up a thirst yelling so much."

Kara and Bobbie giggled, knowing they had sounded a lot like cheerleaders while watching the competition.

"I feel sorry for the horses having to run in such hot weather," Kara said, fanning her face with her hat.

Bobbie agreed with her. "They don't seem to mind it though."

"They're lathered up a bit, but you have to keep in mind that these horses are conditioned for the hot weather, much like athletes are. Sometimes they sweat due to their nervous, high energy," Cody informed them.

They returned to their seats just as the first finalist approached the barrels. The horse bumped one barrel causing it to nearly topple, which would have disqualified the rider. Taking too wide a turn around the barrels can make a difference in hundredths of a second. The woman finished with a slow time.

Hannah was next, charging toward the first barrel in her determination to place first. Her gelding rounded the barrels with ease and agility. Kara could not imagine how a rider remained seated on the horse during those sharp turns. It all amazed her. She still felt they should all get first place. As it was, Hannah was moved to first place as she finished in record time. The crowd was on its feet, cheering for her. She was obviously a well-known favorite.

The last rider fell short of Hannah's time by a few hundredths of a second. First place belonged to Hannah!

How wonderful! thought Kara, as she abruptly realized that she had once again in her excitement unknowingly seized Cody's arm with a firm grip. A bit flustered, she released his arm as though it were on fire, stammering a quick apology.

Cody had noted Kara's excitement when his sister rode and could not help but enjoy the feel of the young widow's hold on his arm—fingernails and all. With a crooked grin, he leaned toward Kara and assured her that he liked friends who showed enthusiasm for life.

Kara acknowledged his remark with a shy smile, her eyes twinkling, thrilled for Hannah's win, the rodeo itself, and the enjoyment of Cody's companionship. The rodeo clown, along with two volunteer cowboys, removed the barrels from the arena, and a rider drove a team of Belgian draft horses inside with an old-fashioned rake to level and smooth the dirt for the next event. A seat above the rake provided a place for the driver who handled the team, expertly maneuvering them around corners and turns.

People stood to stretch. Kara was grateful for the cushions they had brought for comfort on the hard bench. In a short time, the steer-roping competition was ready to begin and folks took their seats again. A cowboy backed his horse into the very corner of a small area next to the calf chute. A rodeo worker put a rope in front of the horse to be certain the horse would not leave the area before the calf was released. If the breakaway was completed before the calf was out, the rider was disqualified. Kara imagined what a challenge it was to keep the horse confined in the small area allotted it. Some reared a little in their excitement to be running. The animals were trained for quick and precise action and speed. The horses appeared more than glad to comply.

One rider after another left the appointed area to pursue the calf across the arena, roping it around the horns, pulling it to the ground, and tying three legs in a required fashion. Each horse was trained to keep the rope taut as the rider dismounted to grasp the calf, flip it on its side, and tie it.

Each spectator, and Kara in particular, cheered with excitement. She didn't know when she had enjoyed herself so much. The competition was stiff; each competitor was more than qualified to be in the arena. Cody was a good source of information for Kara, due to his past experiences in the rodeo circuit and personal acquaintance with the contestants.

Hannah soon joined the foursome after she had cooled down her horse and cared for his needs. Levi had certainly earned the attention.

Bulldogging was next. Once again, a horse and rider entered the small area next to the calf chute, and a cowboy placed the breakaway rope across the entrance. A partner, mounted and positioned on the opposite side of the calf chute, was ready also. A yearling steer was released, and the rider behind the breakaway rope, charged after it. The partner rode on the opposite side of the yearling to keep the animal running in a straight pattern so the other rider could dismount the horse while grasping the horns of the steer, pulling it to the ground, and pinning it for a time. These men had to know what they were doing; they could be trampled under by the hooves of the steer, or gouged by a horn.

Kara shivered with excitement as she watched the riders wrestle steers to the ground. She concluded that there is nothing like watching a rodeo in person. Her friends back east were sure to be as excited as she was when she described the events to them.

Head-and-heel roping was next. Cowboys paired off to compete in this event. Mounted at either side of the chute, they waited for a yearling steer to be released. Pursuing the animal, one rider roped the head and one the heel, or foot. As far as Kara could see, it was challenging to rope the animal from either end. The steer moved constantly and created a genuine challenge for the heeler in particular to get a loop on a leg or foot. The heeler had be particularly careful not to get kicked in the process.

Bareback bronc riding and saddle bronc riding competitions followed. The difference between the two events was that the riders for the latter competition wore saddles with stirrups. From her seat, Kara could easily see the chutes, which were opposite the grandstand. With amazement and respect she observed the cowboys as they exited the large gated chutes on the bare back of the horses as they bucked, holding on to cotton ropes that extended from halters the horses wore. Many of the animals twisted and turned in midair and hit the ground bucking. The cowboys had to ride the horses for eight seconds until the sound of the whistle; then they dismounted the best way they could without being trampled underfoot. Sometimes, a rider would leap onto the rump of one of two horses used in the arena to catch the bucking horses once the riders dismounted.

Bull riding was the grand finale. This was the crowd-pleaser. With awe Kara watched the nearly one-ton bulls buck, twist, and turn, seemingly quite agile for animals that were so powerful, muscular, and mammoth in size.

... Audrey Marr ...

How could any rider stay on such a cyclone? Kara wondered. Then she remembered that this was the type of beast Cody had ridden numerous times not so long ago. She was both delighted and fearful as the riders did their best to ride the bulls for eight seconds. They only item keeping a cowboy on the back of a huge bull was a strap fastened behind the bull's front shoulders. The head and horns were huge! Although the horns were rounded off on the ends to make them blunt, they seemed dangerous and threatening nonetheless. The rodeo clown was constantly working as the cowboys dismounted or fell from the huge beasts. Kara could not envy the riders in the least; she thought them a bit eccentric, shuddering to think what could happen to the men. A few of the cowboys hobbled away. A cowboy had to be mighty tough—or crazy—to enjoy taking this challenge. The prize money was considerable, but Kara felt they had earned every cent.

Before the foursome was ready for it to end, the rodeo was over. A county music band took over, playing from a stage of sorts at the bottom of the grandstand area. Obviously, some attendees intended to dance and enjoy the music. Davey assisted Bobbie down the steps and through the crowd; Cody following suit with Kara, all in pursuit of Hannah, who had left to tend her horse a short time before the rodeo ended. She had invited Kara to meet some of the women who had competed. Kara was more than happy to do so, asking to see Levi as well.

The evening temperature was slightly cooler. Kara and Bobbie both looked attractive with their flushed cheeks and wisps of hair around their face. Davey and Cody were quite pleased to be escorting such fine ladies. Kara wondered what people thought seeing her with the tall rancher. Here she was with a ring on her finger and obviously pregnant.

Well, let them think what they will, she thought. *It's none of their business.*

She was glad for Cody's attentions with so many people milling about in their hurry to get refreshments or take their leave. Casting a sideways glance toward the tall cowboy, she wondered what Cody was thinking. She was surprised Cody was not married with a family by now. She guessed him to be her age, give or take a few years. She noticed that women he knew enjoyed talking to him and giving him their undivided attention. He seemed the type of guy all women like to know—kind, warm, and considerate. He made a person feel as though anything he or she had to say was important to him. This quality appeared to come from his heart, not simply from good manners. She had never noticed him to be bored—or boring—no matter what the conversation.

Kara felt protected with his hand securely on her arm, directing her around and through the crowd. It had been four long months since Jonny was taken from her. She had forgotten what it was like to be touched and handled with this type of care and consideration that Cody was showing. The thought came to her that she could like being with this man if she allowed herself the privilege. But it was too soon, much too soon. She was not certain she would ever be ready to give her heart to another.

Realistically, though, what was she going to do with herself? She could not continue to live with her brother indefinitely. She had to seriously consider her options before too much time passed, but for now she told herself to enjoy her time with friends.

The foursome came upon Hannah as she made a final sweep with the brush on her gelding's coat. She obviously had been taught to take pride in her horse and to give him the best of care. Levi's glossy, mouse-colored coat shone.

Bobbie and Kara stroked the gelding's sleek neck as Hannah introduced a few of her rodeo friends as they passed. The men stood off to the side making small talk.

"Levi seems so gentle, Hannah," Kara said.

"He certainly is," Bobbie agreed. Levi turned his head toward the women with a soft nicker, as though he wanted to say something.

"You're just a big baby, aren't you?" Bobbie questioned the horse softly, turning to pet his head. "You keep up the good work out there in the arena, OK?"

Levi nickered at Bobbie, as though to assure her he would do his best.

Everyone laughed.

"You ladies keep showing such love and affection to my horse, he won't be fit to ride, he'll be so spoiled!" Hannah jested as she caressed the horse's neck. "Then again, with extra loving, maybe Levi will keep up the good work and get us to the nationals."

"His coloring is really unique," Kara observed. "What breed of horse if he?"

Hannah smiled, pleased to note Kara and Bobbie's interest. "He's a *grulla*—a unique name for a rare coloring. It's a Spanish word meaning "crane," because some horses have the bluish-gray color of a blue heron. Levi here has the coloring more like that of a mouse, but the black, dorsal stripe down the middle of his back tells a person he's a *grulla*."

Both women agreed the gelding was beautiful and special indeed.

"I need to get Levi loaded," Hannah said to her friends. "After that, how about all of us going to the local café in town for a bite to eat—my treat."

Since no one could turn down such an offer, the four agreed to follow her into town.

"Great!" Hannah beamed. "I have to wait for my girlfriend to load her horse too, and then I'll be ready to go."

Hannah and her friend shared traveling expenses to rodeos. With good sportsmanship, they were always excited about one another's accomplishments and never allowed competition to interfere with their friendship. They had known each other since high school and had become the best of friends. Jodee Parkinson was also a Christian. This was the real plus in the friendship they shared. Traveling the rodeo circuit was a tough business, involving tough people at times. Jodee had finished with an all-around fourth place, but she was not to be discouraged. There were more rodeos ahead, so she had only to hang in there and work hard. She felt that her horse had not been his best that day, the heat possibly complicating matters.

The air-conditioned café was a relief. The six people enjoyed their time together, each getting better acquainted.

At one point, Jodee said, "Hannah and I attended the Christian cowboy fellowship meeting last night. It was quite interesting."

Cody nodded. "I always liked attending those meetings, even when I wasn't serving the Lord. You know how it can be," he added with a smile, "going to a church fellowship and then living a sinner's life the rest of the week."

"There seemed to be a hunger and a greater interest this time, I think," Hannah explained. "Don't you agree, Jodee?"

"Absolutely! A few of the guys brought out their guitars and another, his fiddle. The message was about how we can be Christians and still enjoy life and live without the guilt of sin."

As conversation continued, Kara concluded that the message was true—her friends had proven that fact time and time again. They knew how to laugh and have fun, and she didn't have to be concerned about being the brunt of a cruel joke. She happily felt comfortable in the group.

The subject changed to rodeos as Hannah and Jodee told the group some of their experiences in the rodeo circuit.

"Jodee, do you remember," Hannah began, "that time we had to present the flags to the crowd?"

Jodee rolled her eyes, smiling.

"I realize it wasn't funny at the time," Hannah explained, placing a comforting hand on her friend's shoulder. "Jodee's horse was feeling frisky and rowdy that evening. As we rode into the arena, her horse acted up some. She was holding and balancing the large flag in the stirrup with one hand while holding the reins in the other. It's difficult to have control of the horse under those circumstances, if the need arises. As we approached the grandstand full of people for the national anthem, her horse decided he'd had enough and started bucking hard. Before I realized it, Jodee was laying flat on her back in the dirt, the flag still in her hand!" Hannah laughed hard as she remembered the incident. "You had to be there to appreciate how embarrassed Jodee was! At the time, everyone was worried she had gotten hurt."

Kara's eyes were wide by the end of the story. "Did you get hurt, Jodee?"

"No, just my pride. There I was, a rodeo competitor, lying in the dirt for all the world to see. I'd taken special care with my clothes and hair too!"

Kara thoroughly enjoyed the adventures of Hannah and Jodee as they continued to share past experiences. At some of the stories, everyone laughed until their sides ached.

"I'm beginning to realize that humor runs in the Ralston family" Kara concluded as she peered at Cody.

Cody rewarded her with a wry grin. "It could be, Kara."

The fun evening had to come to an end sometime. Back home in her bed, following a cool shower, Kara thought back on the full day and decided that she, Davey, and their friends were creating memories that would last a lifetime. With a contented sigh, Kara rolled to her side. She always began by facing the side of the bed where Jonny should have been, her arm extended across the emptiness. A full moon shone through the window. Kara eyed her wedding band glistening in the moonlight. *How long did one wear a wedding band from a beloved mate?* she wondered.

Yet the baby in her womb was Jonny's. She felt obligated to remain true to him for the time being. Maybe she was jumping to conclusions to think about it at all. Should there be a desire for another man first? Any man in general or just one in particular? Why was she thinking such things when the day itself had been nearly perfect? The wondering only made her weary. It was easier to let life happen as it should—one day to a time.

Closing her eyes, she scolded herself, declaring she was not going to allow tears. The hour was late and she needed to sleep. It did not take long for the young woman to do exactly that.

... 19

THE SUMMER DAYS FLEW BY. KARA COULD NOT BELIEVE THAT THE DAY FOR her in-laws to arrive was upon them already. The Madisons had not intended to wait so long before visiting Kara, but one job after another had come up with the nursery and landscaping business they owned. Summer was the busiest time of the year in their line of work. They had chafed at the numerous setbacks to their plans. They continued to call often to check on their daughter-in-law's progress concerning the pregnancy.

Since time was of an essence, the Madisons had chosen to fly out and spend a week or so with Kara, arriving Thursday and departing Saturday of the following week. They had offered to stay at a motel, but Dave would hear none of it. They graciously accepted his invitation to stay at his house, agreeing that the arrangement would make it easier to spend quality time with Kara.

Kara greeted the couple as they entered the airport after disembarking the airplane. Their faces lit upon seeing Kara. Nearly five months pregnant, their daughter-in-law was visibly with child. Alice was thrilled to hug Kara, exclaiming that it was too good to be true and crying with joy for the coming baby. Until she was able to see for herself that Kara was indeed expecting a child, it had not been a complete reality. Jon, too, happily embraced Kara.

A few tears escaped Kara's eyes and rolled down her flushed cheeks. It was wonderful to see two of her favorite loved ones. From all appearances, her in-laws looked as if they were doing well. Since her own parents had passed away several years before, Jon and Alice had dearly become like second parents to her.

"You look wonderful—like the pregnancy agrees with you, Dear."

"Thanks, Alice," Kara returned. "I feel great and try to do all the right things." She had chosen a sleeveless summer dress with a rounded neckline. The light blue color suited her tanned complexion; she looked the picture of health.

Once Jon gathered the luggage, Kara escorted the couple to Bobbie's car. Bobbie had offered to trade vehicles with Kara for the week the Madisons would be in town. The car was definitely a more practical choice than her small truck. Jon had offered to rent a car, but Kara saw no need for it and assured him everyone would get along fine.

Their first stop was to see Davey and Drew at the auto detailing shop. Sandy, who was filling in for Kara while the Madisons visited, was the first to greet the couple. Little Emily Rose was sitting contentedly in the baby swing and playing with her fingers when Kara lifted her from the seat to cuddle and introduce her, expressing the thought that she would not mind having a little girl like her. Jon and Alice marveled at the baby's liquid, brown eyes set in the dark, curled eyelashes. Emily cooed and kicked in delight as they fussed over her.

Dave and Drew entered the office to greet the arrivals. Jon asked to see the shop, while Alice chose to visit with Sandy and Kara, all the while holding the baby. Alice told Emily that she was playing an important role in getting Alice practiced for her new grandchild. Sandy and Kara exchanged smiles. Kara was certain the time with her in-laws would fly by much too fast.

✥ ✥ ✥

Once Jon and Alice were settled in the guest room of Davey's house, everyone gathered in the kitchen to eat a delicious meal Kara had prepared. The little garden was still producing fresh vegetables, to everyone's delight. Beef sirloin stir-fry was on the menu, along with Jell-O salad.

... All Things Become New ...

Kara had so many questions for the Madisons. How was business going? How were Jonny's two brothers, Jaime and Jason doing? How were some of her long-time friends faring? What did people think about her having a baby—finally?

The Madisons were more than happy to answer all her questions. They could see for themselves that Kara had been right. Montana and Dave had been good for their special daughter-in-law. When they had seen her off at the airport following their son's funeral, they had been quite worried about Kara's ability to cope with her loss and grief. The affection Dave and Kara had for each other was a precious relationship. It showed in so many little ways.

Following the meal and clean up, everyone retired to the living room to converse more.

Alice spoke first as she looked upon her daughter-in-law with affection. "Well, my Dear, Jon and I couldn't be happier for you. You look healthy and happy, but I must admit that we are anxious to see you move back home and begin anew."

Kara returned her smile. "Thank you, Alice. I appreciate your love and concern for me. I'm still undecided as to what I want to do. Montana is growing on me, and I have made some wonderful new friends, whom I hope you get to meet soon. I do know I don't care to return to my home without Jonny there. However, I realize the house has been untouched and remains as I left it. Except for a few sentimental items and photos I want to keep, there's nothing else I care about. Without Jonny, most of the belongings and such don't mean all that much to me."

At the mention of Jonny, everyone's eyes brimmed with tears. It was not long before each of the four mentioned at least one memory they had of him. Jonny had always been gregarious, and soon the four were laughing about some of the antics he had pulled.

The Madisons knew Kara was happy, which had been their biggest concern. Nevertheless, having their first grandchild twenty-four hundred miles away was another matter. They would have to be patient. The baby wasn't born yet, and Kara might change her mind after its arrival.

Alice changed the subject to the coming wedding of their second-born son. "Jaime, as you know, is getting married in a couple of months to his high school sweetheart."

Kara's eyes lit up with pleasure at the reminder. "Yes, I think that's wonderful! Jaime has a level head on his shoulders like Jonny did. I wish him all the best!" She thought of her own marriage to her high school sweetheart.

"He always did like the house and neighborhood you live in, Kara," Jon said. "Don't be surprised if he calls to question you about your plans for the house."

It pleased Kara a great deal to think about another family member owning her home. She was sure that it would have made Jonny happy as well.

✥　　✥　　✥

The week was fast-paced, as Kara had carefully planned for her in-law's visit. Drew and Sandy had invited Kara, Dave, and the Madisons for dinner. Since growing up in the same neighborhood as the Madisons, Drew had some questions of his own about people and places. For Drew, as well as Dave and Kara, it was a good time of catching up on news.

Emily warmed everyone's hearts. Jon chose to hold her when he had the opportunity, smiling and cuddling her. "You're a little beauty, Emily!" he informed her after she rewarded him with a toothless smile.

"Kara, if you have one such as Emily, we would be thrilled!" Alice stated, being especially taken with the little girl.

Kara laughed. "She is a darling, isn't she? But I honestly don't mind if I have a boy or a girl. My greatest concern is that this baby is healthy." Kara patted her rounded stomach for emphasis. No one could refute her statement.

As Kara yawned, Davey suggested they all needed their rest. With a promise to visit again before the Madisons' departure, the guests took their leave.

✥　　✥　　✥

Bobbie was included in a few dinners. Kara had taken the Madisons to the floral shop shortly after their arrival to introduce them to her friend, as well as to take note of the professional quality of work Bobbie and her mother did. Jon and Alice took an immediate liking to the young businesswoman and made a purchase. Alice attempted to be subtle with her questions to Davey concerning Bobbie. It was obvious the two were becoming more than friends. Dave would not say much about their relationship, although he hinted to a thing or two.

During the day, Jon and Alice were content to share a quiet breakfast with their daughter-in-law, followed by a drive to town to browse in stores, or to the country to sightsee.

Since Kara had become a friend of the Ralston family, Martin and Rita took the liberty to invite Kara and her in-laws for lunch, requesting that they come early so they would have plenty of time to get acquainted. It had been some weeks since Kara had been to the ranch, so she was grateful for the invitation. She had missed the Ralston family, feeling as though they were an extended family who filled the void in her life caused by the absence of her own parents.

Jon and Alice were impressed with the ranch and the homey, comfortable Ralston house. It was surrounded by huge Cottonwood trees, and it stayed cool and comfortable, even in the warmest weather. Rita escorted her guests to the family room, a pleasant place to sit and chat and sip iced tea. The room contained two welcoming sofas of burgundy leather and two variegated forest-green rugs on the hardwood floor. A huge, stone fireplace was against one wall of the room. A recent addition to the house, the room's walls were made of square logs and chinking. The cathedral ceiling with its four skylights added appeal, as well as lighting, to the room. Stairs against one wall led to an open loft, which was connected to the main house structure. Antiques were scattered throughout the room and simple muslin curtains decorated the windows.

"Rita, how is it that I was never shown this room before?" Kara asked, a curious expression on her face.

"Summer is such a busy time of year. It seems family and friends are going in all directions. We only recently put the finishing touches on this room," Rita answered with a smile. "If it makes you feel any better," she continued good-naturedly, "this is the first time we've had a chance to entertain guests in here, which is the reason this room was created."

"I love it! It's so warm and inviting," Kara said, complimenting various items in the room and praising Rita's talents.

Alice joined in, agreeing with her daughter-in-law.

"Thank you, Kara," Rita said, pleased but modest with the compliments she received.

Rita went to the kitchen to do last-minute preparations for the meal as Martin continued conversing. Jon Madison wanted to hear more about the ranch and its operation, curious to know how things were done in the west, while Martin inquired of both Madisons about the nursery and landscaping business they operated.

Kara decided to help in the kitchen. Rita put Kara to work adding a few items to the dining room table, while Rita finished the main dish preparations. The two chatted like old friends as they went about their duties. Rita called Martin and the guests to the table once everything was in order. After Martin said the blessing over the food, Jon and Alice surmised for the first time that these people must be Christians.

Halfway through the meal, Hannah and Cody entered the house. They had been checking cattle in the mountain pasture and repairing the fence where it was needed. They had healthy summer tans and looked like quite the westerners in jeans and cowboy boots. The brother and sister were a bit breathless in their rush to take their places at the table, eager to get acquainted with the guests.

Kara suddenly felt shy in Cody's presence as he took a chair across from her. She had not seen much of him or Hannah with the busyness of summer, so she was eager to know what had been going on with the two since the rodeo. It warmed Kara's heart to note the entire Ralston family's interest in her in-laws. Hannah had lots of interesting news concerning the rodeo circuit and her friend Jodee. There seemed to be plenty of work on the ranch to keep Cody busy. The spring calves were growing and flourishing under the summer sun. He was pleased with the entire ranching operation.

Hannah turned to Kara with a question, "So, how's your summer been going since I saw you last? I can see the baby is doing nicely. How have you been feeling?"

Kara smiled. "I've been doing fine. And you're right—the baby is doing fine too."

Kara noticed concern and interest on Cody's face as the questions were asked. The coming baby seemed to be an important topic to everyone at the table, and conversation was soon centered on the event.

"I already have a midwife, Hannah, and feel comfortable with her," Kara said with excitement.

Both Madisons raised their eyebrows. This was the first the grandparents-to-be had heard about a midwife.

"There's no cause for worry, Jon and Alice," Rita reassured them. "A number of women I know have had a home birth and did fine. It's becoming a common practice among women in this part of the country who desire a more comfortable and less expensive way of birthing. Besides, the midwives are experienced and take every precaution to assure a healthy and safe delivery."

Alice looked uncertain and hoped Kara would get that idea out of her head. The best place for Kara would be back east, where she would use conventional means for delivery—meaning a hospital and an obstetrician—instead of this back-woodsy, primitive way of birthing. After all, this was their first grandchild, as well as her firstborn son's child. This new concept changed Alice's mind about patiently biding her time until the baby was born. There were still a few days remaining to persuade Kara to return home.

Following the meal, Martin asked if the couple would like to go for a drive around the ranch to see a few of the sights. Jon and Alice expressed their delight at the idea while Kara advised the couple that she would stay behind to help clean up.

Rita would hear none of it. "Hannah, why don't you take Kara with you to check on the water tanks for the stock or something to give her a chance to get out of the house?"

In no time at all, Kara was sandwiched between Cody and Hannah as they drove around the ranch doing odd errands. To help settle the lunch they had eaten, everyone exited the truck when a section of fence needed repaired.

On one stop, Kara, with a wistful expression, gazed across the broad land. She released a slight sigh. "I sure do miss riding. I suppose if I weren't along, the two of you would be horseback riding to do this job."

Hannah and Cody would only smile, as she looked from one to the other.

Feeling slightly exasperated, she informed them, with her chin out, "I'm not a delicate flower or a frail piece of china, you know!"

Both siblings looked at her in obvious doubt. Neither wanted to be responsible for a pregnant woman.

. . . Audrey Marr . . .

Hannah cast a glance toward Cody, carefully weighing her words before speaking to Kara, "I suppose if you had a gentle, predictable horse, you could go horseback riding on short excursions. I've known women to do that, including our mother."

Kara understood Hannah's cautious words and the reason for her hesitancy to make a solid commitment. She was touched by her friend's concern and felt fortunate, thankful for the hundredth time that she had decided to give Montana a try.

Unexpectedly, Hannah blurted out the question that Cody had desired to ask Kara, yet it seemed too personal. "So, do you think you'll go back east with your in-laws or not?"

Kara smiled at her friend as she noticed the serious expression and creased brow. "Well, I hadn't given it much thought really. We've all been on the go so much that my in-laws haven't asked. They might be waiting for the right timing to pop the question. I'm five months along now and still don't feel hurried to make a decision. But if I'm expected to give an answer right now, I would have to say no. I mean, I really like the midwife I've chosen; I'm feeling great and see no reason to be hasty. Since meeting such wonderful people as yourself, I can't imagine leaving you all never to see you again. I came west in my grief, feeling absolutely miserable. Your family and Bobbie reached out to show me nothing but love and understanding. You are my friends for life as far as I'm concerned!"

Hannah felt relieved and satisfied with the answer. "It makes me happy to hear you say that, Kara, but we'd best not get sentimental, or I'm going to start crying." So saying, she pointed to the calves frolicking around the fields, occasionally butting heads with one another in an attempt to spar pretending to be grown and tough.

Further along in their journey, Cody stopped the truck again along the fence and everyone disembarked. While Hannah assisted Cody in fixing fence in a particularly rocky area, Kara, who had been wandering around and admiring the beauty of the day, suddenly heard a hissing noise. Startled by the foreign sound, she looked in the direction she thought it was coming from. Stepping closer to peer among the rocks, a rattlesnake unexpectedly rose above a particular cluster of rocks nearby. Kara stood as though frozen to the spot, her eyes huge with a look of horror on her face, uncertain as to what she should do. It was clear to her the snake was giving warning and not at all happy with someone trespassing.

Cody suddenly stepped in front of her with a .22 pistol and shot the snake dead. Kara jumped at the sound of the gunshot, bringing her out of the numbness. Snakes had never been her favorite creature, and she was certain she had never seen a snake this big.

Cody grasped her arm. "Are you all right?"

Kara could only nod her head in reply.

"You look a bit pale. We're so used to rattlers I hadn't thought to warn you that you might see one. Fortunately, they give you plenty of warning before they ever strike. Are you sure you're OK?"

"Y-y-yes," Kara stammered. "I've never had a liking for snakes, and that was the first rattlesnake I've ever seen! But I'm fine—really."

Studying Kara's face for a moment, he seemed convinced that she told the truth. He kindly suggested they go back to the truck. During the next few stops en route to the ranch house, Kara chose to stay close to her friends. No snake was going to spoil her day entirely, although it did not hurt to be cautious.

Rita greeted them upon their arrival with glasses of cold iced tea. Then she served a Jell-O salad and lemon pound cake.

Jonathan and Alice appreciated the sincerity and warmth of the Ralston family and felt sad when the visit had to come to an end. Martin grasped Jon's hand with a firm grip and smiled, expressing his pleasure in getting to know him, suggesting they should stay in touch. The women exchanged addresses and hugs.

Soon Kara and her in-laws were driving in the direction of Davey's house. He would be home from work presently, and they wanted to get in all the conversation with him that they could.

After a simple meal of taco salad and applesauce, they took a relaxing walk in the woods. It was a pleasant ending to a wonderful day.

✜   ✜   ✜

The day before the Madisons were to depart, they invited Davey and Kara to dinner at a nice restaurant of their hosts' choice as a way of expressing their appreciation for a wonderful time in Montana. It had been some time since they had been able to have a real vacation. Feeling refreshed and rested from their stay, they were eager to get back to work on Monday. Plans had already begun for Jaime's wedding, and Alice was hoping to be involved as much as she could. She spoke fondly of her future daughter-in-law and was eager to help. Both Jon and Alice were confident it was going to be a good match.

Kara and Davey both favored Chinese food, much to the Madisons' delight. At a secluded table in the restaurant, the four placed their orders then discussed the possibility of the Madisons returning to Montana at Thanksgiving or Christmas. Davey extended an invitation to the couple, expressing his pleasure in their company and his desire that they stay at his house any time. Everyone had gotten along well together, and he did hope they would not hesitate to take him up on his offer.

Before long, the waiter brought their steaming dishes of food. With great pleasure and hearty appetites, the four were prepared to enjoy the meal. Struck by a sudden thought, Jon kindly requested that Davey say grace. During his stay in Montana, Jon had grown to appreciate the love and sincerity of the young man seated beside him. He had noticed a distinct difference in Davey and the Ralston men. Jon felt he was falling short of some invisible mark, although he was not sure the reason for it. He only knew he could not deny the quietness and strength that these men possessed, as well as a profound peace.

Along with this realization, he remembered Jonny approaching him about his newfound faith. With pain, he recalled the anger he felt concerning his son's zeal for this Jesus. Jon had had a ready, sharp reply for his son. Jonny was obviously hurt and greatly disappointed by his father's reaction and had not stayed long following the sharp rebuke. However, his father's reaction had not discouraged Jonny's love for him.

The elder Jon was now filled with regret. He saw the same love for this Jesus in Davey and Martin. Even Alice had noticed the difference, acknowledging that the Ralstons were not like any other people they knew. The Madisons had been casually acquainted with Davey because of his relationship to Kara, but he had definitely changed since coming to Montana.

Unknown to the couple, Davey had shared with those in his Bible study his desire that the Madisons would become Christians.

Numerous believers—some of whom the Madisons had never met—were bringing many prayers before God's throne on the Madisons' behalf.

Davey was surprised, yet pleased, to say a blessing over the food. He was both humbled by the request and excited to think that he had been a testimony for the Lord.

Following the prayer, they made small talk. Eventually, the conversation came around to Kara's plans concerning the baby. Kara had known it would. However, she was not upset; she understood and appreciated her in-law's concern for the welfare of the baby, as well as for her. She was prepared to give them an answer.

"I'm aware that you are concerned about the baby and about me, but as of now I have no desire to return to the east. Coming out here to be with my brother has been the best thing for me." Davey rewarded her with an ear to ear grin as she gazed fondly at him. "It's hard to explain what I mean," she continued. "Events have changed my life drastically. At first, I wanted to shrivel up and die, but as time has gone by, I've somehow determined not to be defeated. I've been able to do the things I love, like planting flowers and growing a garden. I've been able to spend many quiet hours alone in the woods or at my favorite place in a chair by my bedroom window. These simple pleasures have somehow been healing for me.

"Being in an entirely different setting has helped me move forward with my life. I couldn't ask for better friends than the ones I've made here. They're caring, loving people who seem to genuinely have my best interests at heart. They've been part of my healing also. I feel most comfortable with the idea of having the baby in Montana. Davey has graciously expressed the freedom for you to visit any time. I understand that this is your first grandchild, and I know it will be hard for you both if I'm not with you. But for now I feel happiest right where I am. I've been too busy to be as miserable as I might have been in my old, familiar surroundings, which has been good for me. Please try to understand where I'm coming from for now, OK?"

Seeing Kara's green eyes pleading for understanding, they could not help but try. With a sigh, Alice looked to her husband, who could only give a shrug of helplessness. In privacy they had discussed this possibility. Kara was sweet, but she also had a stubborn streak. Once she made up her mind to something, it was difficult for someone else to change it. They could not argue the fact that Kara was indeed happy and that this life-style apparently agreed with her.

"Somehow, Dear, I knew you would say those words," Alice said, "though part of me hoped I was wrong. We have no right to interfere in your life, and we know you'll do what's best for the baby. It's just that the thought of you having a baby at home, without the assistance of a real physician is scary. And I was hoping that we'd be around to spoil the baby rotten." Smiling slightly at the last statement, Alice could only shrug.

Kara gently grasped the hand of her mother-in-law to express her love. "Thank you, Jon and Alice, for your support. You know I'm not good with confrontations, and I was hoping I could somehow make you understand. Feeling the baby moving inside me makes me feel most protective of him or her, and I do want what's best for the baby. You know I'd have it no other way. I've waited too long for this. I only wish Jonny were here with the four of us this moment. I want so much to tell him what I'm feeling about the baby and how active the baby is, but Jonny isn't here. Does it ever stop hurting?" Tears pooled in her eyes at her confession.

The Madisons struggled with their emotions too at the mention of their belated son. They knew Kara and their son had cared deeply for one another. They also knew they could depend on her to make the right decision for the baby. Wasn't her happiness what they desired most for Kara?

Davey gently reminded everyone of the time. The Madisons had to catch an early flight. He was as relieved as his sister that things had gone as well as they had. He was especially happy to know that Kara had made a definite decision about her life. It had been a while coming, yet he knew the Lord was not finished with his sister. He had noted on occasion her spiritual hunger, though maybe she herself had not realized it yet. *The Lord is good!* he thought.

At home after the Madisons retired, Davey gave his sister a firm hug and bade her good night as well.

Kara felt relieved that the confrontation was over and her final decision in the open. She was peaceful and confident that she had made the right choice. But, oh, how she missed her Jonny as she stretched out on the feather bed, her arm, out of habit, extended across the vacant place beside her. Wondering how she would ever get along in the future, she suddenly remembered that a scripture said a person should take things one day at a time. Maybe Davey would help her find the verse. An unexpected kick from the baby brought her out of her pensive mood, reminding her that she had more going for her than she realized. Smiling in the darkness, Kara folded her arms over her swelling abdomen and fell into a contented sleep.

✤ ✤ ✤

The day was going to be warm, with clear blue sky and sunshine. As Kara prepared to drive the Madisons to the airport, she knew that saying "hello" had been the happy part; "goodbye" would be difficult.

Both she and Alice cried at the airport. They would truly miss each other. Alice gently asked once again if she would reconsider and return with them, but Kara was sure of herself. With mixed emotions, the Madisons promised to stay in touch as usual and boarded the plane when their flight number was called. Kara reminded herself that it was not as though she would never see them again, and she willed herself to stop crying.

Since Kara had to exchange vehicles with Bobbie, she thought it would be a good time to squeeze in a visit if Bobbie could spare the time.

The hour was still early when Kara arrived at Bobbie's apartment and boldly knocked on the door. Bobbie answered the door, pleasantly surprised to see her friend. She was an early riser, ready to meet the day, while her mother continued to sleep soundly. The week had been busy, with a Friday evening wedding for which she had prepared all the decorations and flowers. Both Bobbie and her mother had agreed to take Saturday off from the floral shop, arranging for a longtime friend to fill in.

"How about going out to breakfast—my treat?" Kara asked.

"How can I refuse an invitation like that?" Bobbie answered with a grin before glancing at her sweat suit. "Let me change into something suitable and you're on. Go ahead and make yourself comfortable while I get ready."

... Audrey Marr ...

As Kara waited, she absently browsed around the room, scanning over the different items decorating the walls. Family pictures were mounted throughout the living room. Bobbie was an only child. Her father and mother were divorced and he was living somewhere in Montana. Kara had always thought it wise to not interfere too much in other people's lives, allowing them the freedom to tell her as much as they wanted to. She had learned while working with so many different people at the bank that each person had different problems and struggles. At least Bobbie had her mother, and they appeared to have a special mother-daughter relationship.

Soon Bobbie was ready. Noting Kara's red nose, she surmised it had been a sad parting.

"I'll drive," Bobbie offered as they went outside. "How did the send-off go? Did your in-laws have a good time while they were here?"

"I'll fill you in over breakfast. Right now I'm starving!"

The two women laughed. Having an appetite had never been a problem for Kara, but the pregnancy had definitely increased how often she wanted to eat. She was feeling good about the fact that thus far she had only gained ten pounds. She tried to eat light between meals, snacking on fresh fruits and vegetables, but right now she craved a solid breakfast. Her stomach had felt too fluttery earlier to have an appetite, but now that the goodbyes had been said, she was ready to eat. She suggested a particular restaurant that met with Bobbie's approval.

At the restaurant, the women quickly filled their plates at the breakfast buffet and got comfortable after Bobbie said grace. Kara was thankful to have someone else willing to bless the food.

After a few minutes of serious eating, Bobbie broached the subject of the visit once again. "So, how did it go with your in-laws?"

Kara had just taken a bite of waffle. She held up an index finger. Then, ready to begin, she looked up to see Hannah Ralston entering the restaurant. Spotting Kara and Bobbie at about the same time, Hannah approached their table.

Kara was genuinely pleased to see her dear friend. She had not had a chance to really visit with Hannah and have some girl talk at her house. "Hannah! Please sit with us. We haven't had much time to chat with so much going on between your activities and mine."

"Are you sure? I didn't come here intending to crash your breakfast. I've been on the road since three this morning and I'm starved. I decided to take a break and eat here before going home."

Bobbie was glad to see the young woman too. The three had much in common, including their age. "You do look tired, Hannah. How's the rodeo circuit?"

"It's OK. About this time of year, a person gets a bit tired going here and there to compete. I think my horse, Levi, takes it all in stride a lot better than I do." Turning to peer at Kara, she asked, "How did it go with your in-laws? They appeared to be enjoying themselves when they visited the ranch."

"I was just getting ready to explain everything to Bobbie when you came along, so now I can begin," Kara said with a smile. "Actually, it was a good time together. They were pressuring me some to return home with them, but I told them that with Jonny gone, I felt I needed a fresh start. Coming out here to be with Davey has been a godsend. I do need to return to the east for a visit. I have to sort my personal items and decide what to keep and what to do with the rest. My two brothers-in-law and Jonny's parents will be happy to help as much as they can."

"I guess your in-laws weren't very happy with your decision. I mean, it is their first grandchild and all," Hannah said.

"Yes, I do feel bad about that, but they're only a plane trip away. Davey and I both made it clear that they are always welcome here, and of course I'll plan trips back east as well. Fortunately, they are not the kind of people to harass a person too much, and they seemed to respect my decision once they realized that I was happy. We were also able to share some of our fondest memories about my husband. It felt good to laugh and cry together."

"Is it getting any easier for you, Kara?" Bobbie asked, her sapphire blue eyes showing concern. "They say time is a healer. Is that true?"

Cocking her head to the side, Kara replied, "Yes, I suppose it is beginning to be. Maybe it's because of the baby and all. I don't know . . . I still miss Jonny a lot. I wish he were here to share those little things about expecting a baby that only a husband and wife can appreciate, but there's nothing I can do about the circumstances that have come about, so I'm out to make the best of the situation. And I have to say that if it weren't for the two of you, things would have been even more difficult for me. Words aren't enough to express how I really feel about you both. Now, that's all I can say for now because I'm going to get sentimental and start crying and I'll blubber too much to eat and I'm hungry!"

The three laughed and agreed they should enjoy the meal. The baby was the next topic. Bobbie asked about childbirth classes.

Kara's expression was blank. "I hadn't given it any serious thought, although it might be a good idea. I would need a coach, preferably a woman."

Hannah and Bobbie blurted out simultaneously that they would love to be her coach. Each looked at the other, surprised that they had both spoken in unison and burst into laughter.

"Oh, my! I'm tired and giddy, I think," Hannah gasped.

"Hannah, you're so funny!" Bobbie interjected.

"Well, maybe you both can be some help, possibly taking turns—one will coach me while the other tries to soothe my brother's distraught nerves. I can't imagine what he's going to be like when it comes his turn to be a father instead of an uncle. He's ridiculous when it comes to this baby, talking about all the things he's going to do with him or her. I have to keep reminding him that I need to get on with my life and eventually find a place of my own. He did make me promise that I wouldn't do anything until after the baby is born, so that much I have agreed to." Kara looked directly at Bobbie and continued, "I already feel as though I've taken too much of his time and that has interfered with your relationship with him."

Bobbie could feel the red creeping up her neck and face as she shrugged, as if to say she wasn't sure it mattered.

Kara noticed her friend's discomfort and turned her attention to Hannah. "Speaking of relationships, I've never asked you, Hannah, if you have a man in your life."

"No, not really. There doesn't seem to be a lot of choices out there at the moment as far as men are concerned. One of the bull riders seems to think we could have something going, but I want a Christian man for a husband and this guy doesn't fit the bill. I figure that it'll happen in the Lord's good time. Of course, my parents like to throw hints now and then that they would like to have grandchildren. I often wonder why that is, that parents are only thinking about grandchildren?"

"Now, Hannah, you know your parents love you and want to see you happy. There are so many unhappy relationships out there, I'm certain they're glad you haven't been in a hurry to marry. A broken marriage is a painful thing. I saw a few among my co-workers and was always thankful it wasn't me going through it."

"You're right, Kara," Hannah agreed, with a rueful grin. "I get to feeling lonely sometimes is all. Patience isn't a strong virtue of mine." She scooted her chair out from under the table. "I need to head home. Mom will be looking for me. Stay in touch, OK?"

Kara and Bobbie chose to leave as well, walking with Hannah to the parking lot, where they parted. Kara suggested the two of them could do some shopping before returning to the apartment, but Bobbie declined with the excuse that she had household chores to do, thanking Kara for breakfast. Once at the apartment, Kara promised to see Bobbie again soon and got into Davey's light truck.

Next she decided to visit Sandy and spend time with Emily. However, when she knocked at Sandy's door, there was no answer. *Probably out shopping or something*, Kara thought. This would give her the time to complete some household chores of her own and fix lunch for Dave, who planned to be home by noon.

Davey was able to arrive home early as planned. Kara had sandwiches and potato salad ready to serve. After the two seated themselves at the kitchen table and Davey gave thanks for the meal, he said, "I wondered if you'd like to go on a picnic tomorrow afternoon? It's supposed to be a pleasant enough day, and I have a special place in mind."

The idea appealed to Kara, her green eyes sparkling. The two made plans as to what they should pack. Davey confessed there were some others involved. He and Kara were to provide salad and chips and salsa. With a twinkle in his eyes, Davey added, "I think you had better wear slacks tomorrow."

When Kara questioned him, he refused to say more, causing her to become increasingly curious about what was going on. Realizing she was not going to get an answer, she decided to play along with her brother.

Davey had a few odd jobs outside he wanted to do, and Kara had some correspondence to catch up on.

The day finished up uneventfully as the two enjoyed one another's company. Both chose to retire early. The next day being

. . . Audrey Marr . . .

Sunday, Davey had decided to go to the early church service and be home by 10:30 A.M. Within the last month, the church had chosen to add a second service, one before Sunday school. There had been a gradual increase in attendance with the arrival of a new pastor a year or so before. The church had chosen two services to handle the increase, rather than building a larger church. The new program was working well, and most seemed pleased with the arrangement since the church was not as congested. It was nice to get home earlier and have time to relax and enjoy a full day off from work.

While her brother was attending church, Kara thought it would be a good time to catch up on her Bible reading. She had not gone to the Wednesday night Bible study because of her in-law's visit. Upon Kara's request, Davey had given her the Scripture verses studied. Sitting in her favorite chair by the bedroom window, she recognized that she sincerely missed attending the Bible study and was looking forward to seeing everyone again. Soon Kara was reading further in the Scriptures than what Davey had provided. Once, glancing at the clock on her nightstand, she could not believe how time had flown! She had made the salad, but she had a few chores to complete before her brother returned.

Scurrying around as best she could considering her pregnancy, she quickly finished the picnic preparations. Davey returned and seemed anxious to leave immediately. A bit breathless with exertion as well as excitement, she informed him that she would be ready as soon as she changed her clothes. She was eager to wear her new bib denim overalls. Choosing a maternity blouse of blue cotton, she dressed and tied her Roper shoes then quickly French-braided her hair. The picture she portrayed in the mirror on her bedroom door was that of a healthy, tanned, pregnant young woman. What Kara saw pleased her. She actually looked happy. Well, why shouldn't she be? She certainly had a lot going for her, surrounded by so many who loved her.

Kara was brought out of her pondering by Davey, who was calling her name as he passed through the house to the kitchen to retrieve the cooler and place it in the Blazer. My, but he seemed in a hurry!

At first Kara thought they were going to the Ralston's ranch, but then Davey made a few unfamiliar turns and she was totally

... All Things Become New ...

confused. She obliged her brother to humor him, refusing to ask questions as to their whereabouts after noticing his rather smug expression.

Forty-five minutes later Kara realized where they were. It was the Ralston ranch! Davey had chosen to approach the ranch from the opposite direction just to confuse her.

The entire Ralston family poured out of the house, eager to see the brother and sister, acting as though it had been months since seeing them.

Martin suggested, with a gleam in his eyes, that they take a look at something in the corral before lunch. Kara was a bit perplexed by everyone's behavior. They acted as though there was a secret that everyone was in on except Kara.

In a nearby pasture, Kara could see a mare and her young colt, which Cody had been working with since its birth in the spring. The colt had grown considerably since Kara had last seen him.

Nearing the corral, Kara recognized the various horses that she had come to know by name. She noticed one she had not seen before. A paint gelding walked toward the group as though desiring to be petted, his shiny bay-and-white coat glistening in the sun. The horse had been obviously well cared for. Kara took an immediate liking to him.

Grinning, Martin asked, "Do you like him?"

Kara was quick to respond with a hearty, "Yes! He's beautiful."

Davey stood alongside Kara and draped his arm across her shoulders. "He's all yours, if you like him."

Kara was not sure she had heard correctly, but the grin on her brother's face told her she had not imagined it. With a squeal of delight, she gave her brother an affectionate, firm hug, along with many thanks. Davey confessed the Ralstons had helped. He had only to come up with the money. The rest of the responsibility of owning a horse was hers.

Kara turned her attention to the family. It was clear by the undisguised pleasure on each face that they delighted in seeing others happy. Beside herself with joy, Kara walked to the corral railing to pet the gelding. "Does he have a name?"

"His name is Rebel," Hannah said drolly, "but his name belies his personality. He's gentle and dependable. Dave realized how much you miss riding horses, and we all feel confident this one will be perfect for you, even during your pregnancy. This guy is totally soundproof for sure. We've had him two weeks and tested him every way we could to be sure he was completely safe to ride."

"When can I ride him?" Kara asked, her eyes bright and shining with anticipation.

"Not until after we eat," Rita said in a practical "mom" fashion.

Reluctantly, Kara walked with the others to the house, wishing they had waited until after the meal to show her the horse. In their anticipation, they could not have waited that long though. She conceded to eat, knowing the horse was not going anywhere unless he was led—and she was hungry!

Kara noticed Cody teasing Davey about something. He sure was good looking, and always kind and considerate of others. She was happy to know these precious people. She boldly approached the young rancher to ask if they were going for a horseback ride so she could try out her new mount.

Cody, purposefully putting her off, pretended he couldn't hear her over the growling of his stomach. Hannah encouraged Kara to slap her brother a good one and then she explained that everyone would be riding today.

It sounded wonderful to Kara. The sooner the meal was eaten, the sooner they could get out to the corral.

Everyone chose to eat lighter than usual so they could enjoy their ride. Rita liked to ride horses but was generally too busy and pressed to fulfill other obligations. She was involved in a few church and community activities, which took a lot of time. However, today she informed her family she was grateful to be taking a break to go riding with them.

Martin and Cody saddled the horses quickly and offered Kara a wooden box to mount her horse. She had to suffer some minor teasing from Davey, but Rita encouraged her to not pay attention to her brother because being pregnant was a wonderful blessing, even if it was a bit awkward.

Martin and Rita took the lead, the rest following. The skies were beginning to cloud up, but it did not appear as though it would rain soon.

Rita had not been in the mountains for some time. She appreciated the beauty and quietness the woods afforded. She especially enjoyed the place Cody had taken his sister and friends to earlier in the summer. She always remembered the pungent, piney smell in the coolness of the trees. It was a warm enough day, so the cooler temperatures of the higher elevation felt good. With the progression of summer, everything tended to become brown and dry for lack of rain. Yet here in the trees, it was still green and refreshing. A fair amount of grass remained.

Kara sincerely enjoyed her mount. *Rebel,* she thought. *What a poor choice for his name! He is a gentleman as far as I'm concerned.*

Now and then he cocked an ear her direction to listen to her voice. Kara was certain they were going to be great friends. Everyone was careful to walk his or her horses slowly so Kara would not feel hurried or uncomfortable. Once in the trees, Martin proposed they dismount and walk to stretch their legs a bit. Kara knew this was for her benefit and appreciated his thoughtfulness. It had been a while since she had last ridden; she would have to get used to it again. It was difficult to transfer her additional weight in the saddle.

They walked ten minutes to get the kinks out and remounted once again.

After an hour or so, Martin and Rita turned in the direction of the ranch. They mutually agreed to let the young people continue on. Kara wanted to visit the cave they had explored on their camping trip, and everyone remaining enthusiastically agreed. Hannah took the lead, excited about the prospect of once again seeing one of her favorite haunts.

In the shuffle, Kara found herself riding alongside Cody.

"How do you like Rebel?" he asked with a smile.

"Oh, he's wonderful! I would have no idea how to go about buying a horse, but someone made a good choice getting him for me. I don't suppose you know to whom I should give the credit?" She had the distinct feeling it was Cody who had been responsible for finding the horse. Hannah had been too busy traveling and riding the rodeo circuit.

Cody's answer proved her right, much to her satisfaction. "Well, I guess you could say I am responsible. When Dave approached us about getting you a mount of your own, Dad made a few suggestions and I followed up on them. I was fortunate enough to happen upon Rebel here."

"You have excellent knowledge and taste where horses are concerned, Cody. He's a real beauty. I sincerely appreciate your willingness to help Davey for my benefit."

Cody was gratified with Kara's happiness. The million-dollar smile she gave him nearly melted any resolve he had about waiting patiently to see which way the wind would blow concerning the young widow. He had best watch himself. Fortunately, they arrived at the cave in a few minutes.

Being closest to Kara, Cody hurried to her to help her dismount. She was much too excited about another exploration to realize it would not hurt to be a bit more careful in her condition. No one could fault her though. The other three were as excited as Kara. At the cave entrance, Cody cautioned the others with a mischievous look in his eyes that they should make lots of noise and talk loud so as to scare off any ghosts. Kara would hear none of it and neither would Hannah. They boldly entered the cave, eager to look about. The two women were so engrossed in conversation they failed to notice Davey hiding in the semi-darkness of the cave. Jumping from the shadows and growling, he was promptly rewarded with shrieks of terror followed by a punch on the arm and a poke to the ribs. Immediately covering his ears, he regretted having scared them.

As the women ran into the larger room in the cave, Cody could only laugh at his friend. "That'll teach you to go around scaring those two. I could've warned you about my sister. As a matter of fact, I thought you would've known better where you own sister was concerned."

Davey could only grin, rubbing his ribs in slight exaggeration of injuries sustained during the attack.

The two men joined the ladies by the small bowl of water and conversed a few minutes. While Kara and Hannah splashed the cool water on their faces to refresh themselves, Cody mentioned they should head for the ranch. He had noticed before entering the cave that the skies looked slightly forbidding and the wind had picked up. He knew none of them were prepared for rain should they get caught in a storm. It was not feasible to hurry for home with Kara in her present condition. He decided he would rather spend the night in the cave than take the chance of endangering her—or anyone else for that matter.

... All Things Become New ...

In single file, the four exited the cave, only to be met with an angry, windy sky. Everyone picked up the pace as they realized they must get back to the house as soon as possible. Cody's greatest concern was for Kara, not because he thought she was fragile but because he did not want to take any risks that would endanger her or the baby.

Rebel was as steady and sure-footed as they come. He seemed to sense that his rider was somewhat nervous, so he was patient. They had hardly begun their trek toward home when drops of rain began falling. Cody happened to have a slicker tied to the back of his saddle which he offered to Kara. She thanked him, grateful for his consideration and thoughtfulness. Hannah also had a slicker. The men had to endure the rain until reaching home. Time seemed to crawl. Kara was extremely weary and chilled by the time the ranch house came into view. As Cody helped her from the horse, she grasped his arm for support, her teeth chattering, and her rubbery legs wobbly from the long ride and the cold.

Cody and Davey took the horses to the barn while Hannah assisted Kara to the house. Rita was anxiously waiting at the door to usher them into Hannah's room for dry clothes, clucking and fussing over Kara as if she were her own daughter. A hot shower sounded inviting, but Kara was too weary to put forth the effort. Noticing her fatigue, Rita loaned Kara one of her husband's sweatshirts and sweatpants. Using the tie at the waist, Kara adjusted the pants to fit.

Rita then offered steaming mugs of tea to the women as they plopped on the sofa in the new family room. Kara and Hannah were still chilled when Rita presented them each an afghan to bundle in, concern showing on her face as she studied Kara. With the onset of the storm, Martin had started a fire in the fireplace to warm the house and rid it of the dampness. Sipping the hot beverage, Kara could feel the warmth gradually seeping into her bones again. Davey and Cody were both soaked to the skin and chilled by the time they got to the house. A hot shower did wonders for them. Being about the same size as Cody, Davey was able to borrow dry clothes to wear.

Upon entering the family room, Cody and Davey approached Kara to be sure for themselves she was all right. Snuggled down in the afghan, Kara wished more than anything she could take a nap. Davey nudged his sister. She assured him with a weary smile that she was fine—that the warmth was making her sleepy. She had stayed mostly dry under the slicker, but the wind had seemed to go right through her. Riding back in the rain she had felt queasy, but she did not want to concern her brother with that information. Satisfied that she truly was fine, Davey chose a chair near the fireplace and chatted with Cody, while Kara and Hannah catnapped on the sofas.

Kara continued to sleep as the others went to the dining room to eat. Rita assured Dave she could eat when she awoke. When everyone had finished eating, Rita asked Cody to check on Kara on his way to the bedroom for a book. Since Kara was beginning to stir, Cody knelt in front of her to ask if she was hungry.

The surroundings seemed to spin as Kara opened her eyes and tried to focus. She quickly closed them again, hoping it would stop. She felt disoriented, until she noticed Cody kneeling beside her.

Cody was thinking she looked a bit pale as she opened her eyes again and smiled weakly. "Are you all right?" he asked, his brows knit together.

"I'm not sure. Maybe I'm hungry is all," Kara quickly replied, the dizzy spell subsiding.

"Mom wanted me to see if you were awake and had an appetite. Are you sure you're OK? You're looking sort of pale, if you ask me."

Even though she was not feeling well, Kara felt the warmth of his piercing blue eyes studying her. She hurried to get up without answering him, wondering if her discomfort showed on her face. The room began spinning again, causing her to quickly take a seat again.

Observing Kara's shaky hand as she covered her eyes, Cody placed a hand on her arm. "I think you had better stay where you are and let met bring you some food."

The way she was feeling, Kara was not about to argue with him.

Cody returned with Mom in tow. Rita felt Kara's forehead, fussing all the while, suggesting that a bowl of soup would do her good if she was up to it.

Kara bravely put on a front before them all, not wanting to be the center of attention. She gratefully accepted the bowl of soup on a tray and proceeded to eat, her stomach beginning to churn after the final bite. Rita departed with the empty bowl, pleased that Kara had eaten something.

... All Things Become New ...

Kara suddenly covered her mouth. Cody had been expecting this very thing and was ready with a wastebasket, just in case. Much to Kara's relief, he shoved the container in her hands, just as she vomited. The room was spinning again. She felt awful, wishing she had not eaten after all. How embarrassing!

Cody called for Hannah, feeling helpless and beside himself. He knew such matters were beyond him. Seeing Kara ill alarmed him; he wondered if she and the baby were OK. *Maybe the ride was too much for her,* he wondered and began feeling guilty all over again at her discomfort.

Hannah scurried into the room to hold Kara's hair out of her face as she vomited again. Hannah sent Cody for a cool washcloth. Davey and Rita entered the room about then to observe the situation.

"I can tell you right now," Rita stated, "that your sister isn't going anywhere. She should stay with us until she feels better. Rest and some care are what she needs. Since you have to work, it would be for the best. Hannah has a spare bed in her room and can help when needed for a few days before she goes on the road again."

"I certainly can't argue with you, Rita," Davey said in surrender. "I appreciate your help; I'm not very good as a nurse maid."

"Most men aren't," Rita said dryly, smiling.

Kara felt too ill to care about any plans they were making for her. Any bed sounded wonderful to her right now. Davey helped Kara to the bedroom. Then the women took over, getting Kara settled into bed with a bucket close by. All Kara wanted to do was sleep.

… 20

THE NEXT DAY KARA WAS MISERABLE. SHE WAS TOO ILL TO WORRY MUCH about the baby. Rita tried to push fluids as much as she could, encouraging Kara to drink some ginger ale to help settle her stomach. Hannah was always close by to help Kara to the bathroom. It was surprising how much she could sleep.

Cody hovered nearby when work on the ranch did not keep him away. He was alarmed that something worse might befall the young woman. "I didn't know someone could sleep so long, Mom!" he finally blurted out in his anxiety, standing in the middle of the kitchen looking much like a helpless boy.

Rita attempted to put his mind at ease. "Rest is the best thing for Kara. There is nothing to worry about." She gave her son a reassuring pat on the back while passing him on her way to the kitchen sink. "The baby is fine. One thing about babies –they are made of tougher stuff than people realize. They're even somewhat greedy, taking from the mom what they need to continue growing and remaining safe in the womb."

Rita smiled inwardly at the helplessness of a man when it came to an illness or a crisis in the house. He could handle a one-hundred-pound calf, rope and brand cattle, and do all manner of ranching duties, but heaven forbid even they should become ill!

Rita could not help but notice the special concern her son had for Kara. In fact, the entire Ralston family could tell that for some time now Cody's feelings had run deeper than he admitted. They sent up many prayers for Cody and Kara.

Yet, Cody was not the only guilty party. They all cared deeply for Kara. She had woven her way into each of their hearts. They were thankful to know she was seeking the Lord, though maybe she was not aware of the fact yet. Prayer was the best thing they could do for her right now, as well as show Christ's love.

The following morning, Kara began thinking she might live. She felt up to eating something light. Pleased to see her looking a bit perky, Hannah offered to get her tea and toast.

Kara was sure she looked a mess, deciding she would have to ask her hostess for a brush when Hannah returned. Just then, much to Kara's horror, Cody appeared in the bedroom doorway, knocking lightly before entering. Quickly covering her head with a blanket, she pleaded with him, "Oh, Cody, please go away until I'm more presentable!"

The young rancher was amused by her reaction. "It seems to me you weren't concerned whether or not I was around the past day or so. Hannah told me you felt up to eating something, but I had to see this for myself. I guess if you're so concerned about appearances, you really are fine."

Kara snatched a pillow from the bed and attempted to throw it at him, but it fell short of its mark. Goodness! What a weakling she was!

Cody cast her a look of mock shock and horror, retrieving the pillow from the floor before stepping beside the bed to gently tuck the pillow behind Kara's back.

There was that certain look in his eyes again. She was a bit shy at his close presence and felt relieved to see Hannah enter with a tray. Cody left, a smile playing on his lips.

"I brought you your favorite herbal tea, if I remember right, and toast. If you can keep this down, I'll consider bringing you some soup."

"Thanks, Hannah." Taking a sip of tea as though it were gourmet, Kara heaved a contented sigh. "Ummm, blackberry tea is my favorite, you remembered right! It's wonderful."

Kara made the toast and beverage disappear quickly, while Hannah tidied the bedroom, fluffed the pillows behind Kara's back, and smoothed the blankets.

"Wow, Hannah, you have a real gift of hospitality. I appreciate it."

"Moms have quite an impact on their children," Hannah replied, grinning. "Now, how about getting out of bed for a spell and soaking up some sun rays?"

"That would be great!"

Taking a bathrobe from a hook behind the bedroom door, Hannah helped Kara get presentable and then brushed her hair. Kara felt quite pampered.

Walking sounded easy, but Kara felt as though her legs were made of rubber. Feeling weak as a baby after lying around so long, she was almost giddy. She giggled so much that Hannah soon joined in while trying to assist her to the deck at the back of the house.

Cody came upon this scene after entering the house to get his notebook containing information about the cattle. He easily lifted Kara into his arms and carried her to the back deck as Hannah instructed. Gently depositing her on a lounge chair, he tipped his cowboy hat toward Kara and walked away.

All of this left Kara rather speechless and somewhat embarrassed with her behavior. What must he think of her? Actually, she thought he knew her well enough that it probably didn't bother him as much as it did her. So why should she make an issue of it?

Hannah covered Kara with a light blanket to ward off any chill and left her alone with a few magazines. Kara did not care to look at the magazines with the lovely view of the mountains before her. From her vantage point, she could also see a good portion of the ranch. She noticed Cody and Martin leaving the main ranch on horseback. The father and son seemed to get along so well. Mr. Ralston, Sr. was a sweet and respectable man. And his son? Cody reminded her a lot of Jonny, yet Cody was also very different in his unique way. If she could chose to marry again, she found Cody to be someone she would consider.

The direction of her thoughts startled her. However, being only twenty-five years old, could she continue as she was—widowed and alone—for years and years to come? Kara pondered the question as she absentmindedly toyed with the wedding band on her

. . . All Things Become New . . .

finger. She felt that if Jonny could have a say, he would want her to be happy. Being permanently single with a child to raise was not appealing to her. Besides, she did want another home of her own somewhere, and she certainly wanted more than one child, if possible. Most importantly, she truly desired a companion and friend, someone who would love and cherish her and grow old with her. Deciding she was too weary to resolve her personal problems, Kara settled into the chair to catnap. Soon she was asleep.

Suddenly, Jonny was in the distance, standing on a beach. She could see his familiar face so clearly. But wait—she was in a boat. Why was she in a boat? She had never cared for boating or for deep water. After nearly drowning as a young child, she had a phobia about water, if she were honest enough to admit it. Contemplating her next move, her husband unexpectedly spoke to her, pleasure and love written on his face, "Kara!"

"Jonny, how I've missed you! What should I do? You know I don't like boating and—well, what are you doing over there?"

Instead of answering, Jonny turned and spoke to a man standing beside him. Kara did not recognize the man. He had long hair, a beard, and a long, white, flowing robe. He shone with a brilliant light. The man shook his head. Jonny's shoulders slumped, as if he were distressed and bearing a heavy, invisible load on his back.

The boat had moved closer to the shore, close enough that Kara could see tears glistening on her husband's cheeks. She called his name as loudly as she could, but Jonny did not seem to hear her as he continued to look discouraged and defeated. Kara looked to the bearded man for an explanation. He too had tears in his eyes. She had never seen such love and compassion in a person's eyes as she did in this man's dark eyes. They seemed to pierce her to the core of her soul. She felt exposed and scared, as if he knew everything there was to know about her, as if her soul lay bare before him.

When he finally spoke, showing her the scars on his hands, she knew who He was. "It was for you that I died."

The young woman began weeping as she had never wept before in her life, covering her face to hide the shame, guilt, and grief she felt. Not even when her loved ones had died had she cried as she did now.

Kara suddenly looked up, almost blinded by tears, to see Jonny and the man with their backs toward her, walking away. Panic rising in her, she yelled as loudly as she could. "Jonny, please wait! Jesus, I know who you are. Please don't leave me! I don't want you to go!" The two men continued walking away, as though they didn't hear her.

Kara became hysterical, screaming her husband's name. When he failed to respond, she looked at the water surrounding the boat. Her throat constricted with sheer terror at the dark water all around her, the men becoming more distant. She had to go to them! She wanted to tell Jesus she was sorry and that she didn't hate Him. She knew she needed Him more than ever. Debating what to do, she decided to boldly jump into the water, even though she had never been a good swimmer. The shore was not far away, and she was desperate to get to the men and make them understand.

As the cold water enveloped her, she surfaced, gasping for air. In her fear, she stretched her foot to find the bottom of the lake, but there was no solid footing. Her pregnancy caused her to be cumbersome, weighing her down even more. Quickly tiring, she knew she could not tread water much longer as she called out to Jonny for help. Going under twice in her exhaustion, she surfaced to call on the name of Jesus, pleading for mercy for her and her baby. She did not want to die this way and to lose the baby too!

As though coming out of dark waters that enveloped her, Kara woke from her dream—or had it been a nightmare? Sobbing and wrapping her arms around herself, she felt helpless, overwhelmed, and lost.

Hannah came charging from the house as she heard Kara's sobs, praying that the baby was OK. "Kara, what is it?" In a panic, Hannah grasped Kara's arms. "Talk to me! Is it the baby? Please talk to me!"

Kara wailed hysterically in such loud volume that she did not seem aware of Hannah's presence or her surroundings. It was as though she were locked in a solitary place where no one could reach her.

Hannah gave Kara several firm shakes to bring her out of her stupor, all the while calling her name. Kara suddenly recognized Hannah kneeling beside her. With a strength borne only of terror, Kara grasped her friend's shoulders, begging her for help. She didn't know how to make Jesus understand that she recognized her need for Him!

The alarm on Hannah's face was quickly replaced by surprise and then delight at the young widow's request. She had no idea what had prompted Kara to react this way, but she knew how to help.

Rita Ralston had heard the commotion on the back deck and had come to investigate. She found Kara with a flushed, tear-streaked face and Hannah with a confident and delighted smile, her arms around Kara.

"Mom, would you please get my Bible on the nightstand in my room?"

Rita, with the wisdom of a woman who has lived some years, surmised the scene before her, quickly leaving to do Hannah's bidding. She returned somewhat breathless in her excitement, the Bible in her hand.

Both women shared scriptures with Kara, explaining that man was born to sin and Christ had died so that man can be saved. Once they were confident she understood what they were saying, they asked if she would like to pray. Kara knew without a doubt that she had been on a journey in her life to come to this place in time. It was a pilgrimage that only she could take. No one else could make the decision for her. Recognizing her need for a Savior, she asked Him to forgive her of her sins and to take her as she was, to be molded into His likeness.

By the time Kara was finished, all three were crying. Both Rita and Hannah rejoiced out loud that another soul had entered the Kingdom. Kara now understood how her baby must feel in the womb, so safe and protected. A peace that she had never known filled her being and surrounded her like a cloud.

Following conversation to encourage the young woman, Kara felt emotionally drained and desired rest. Rita and Hannah each took a side to escort her to bed. It was nearly time for dinner, but Rita assured her that there was nothing to worry about; rest was more important right now.

Martin and Cody returned to the house for dinner to find Rita and Hannah awaiting their return. They both talked at once in their excitement. Martin raised his hands for silence and order. He was not alarmed; he could tell it was good news. Turning to his wife of many years, he asked for an explanation. Rita complied by telling of Kara's salvation.

... Audrey Marr ...

Neither Martin nor Cody had expected the news, their eyes wide with the wonder of it all. Once the idea had settled in Martin's mind, he grinned broadly, rejoicing and praising the Lord along with the women. Cody was more reserved in his reaction. He had held himself in check for so long where Kara was concerned; all he wanted to do was to be alone and absorb all that had transpired. He smiled and agreed that it was indeed an answer to prayer and a great way to end the day. The women did not have many details about what had prompted Kara to make the decision, but they were sure she would explain everything when she felt ready.

Cody was relieved that Kara had not yet awakened by the time dinner was over. Making some excuse about checking the pasture, the young rancher excused himself. He felt drawn to his favorite spot. The pond had a calming effect as he sat on the same flat rock he had visited a few months ago. Trying to soak in the quiet solitude, Cody found himself rather unsettled about the news of Kara's conversion. He wondered what would happen next. It nearly took his breath away to see the hand of God move so quickly. Once he had committed everything to the Lord, look what had happened in God's timing! It was almost too good to be true! This meant nothing in the way of a relationship with Kara, yet his heart had sincerely been burdened for the woman.

The Lord had brought circumstances about thus far, so Cody needed to continue to trust Him for whatever the future brought. The past several months of dealing with emotions new to him had been stressful. Cody felt both overwhelmed by and in awe of such a wondrous, loving God. He had to admit to being fearful of the future. No one wants to be hurt. He expressed himself to God in the only way he knew. Resting his head on his arms, he wept deep, heart-wrenching sobs that came from what seemed the very depths of his soul. He knew the Lord understood.

... 21

Kara woke feeling—how did she feel? Peaceful and, oh, so happy! Thinking about her newfound faith thrilled her to the tips of her toes. No longer did clouds of darkness surround her. Life seemed to take on new meaning. Her surroundings looked brighter and more wonderful than she had noticed before. The wonder of it all! She lay in bed, delighting in the new sensation, feeling nothing but contentment.

Hannah happened upon the scene and said, "Well, if you don't look rather happy—almost like the cat who swallowed the canary."

Feeling smug as though she had made a new discovery that only she knew, Kara could only respond with a broad smile.

"Do you think you could eat something? Soup is simmering on the stove."

Food was not something Kara had considered until the mention of the word. Surprise showed on her face with the realization that she was hungry. "Yes, come to think of it—I feel starved!"

"You didn't think you could continue as you have been the past few days, did you? I'm sure that little one requires something more," Hannah grinned. "Here or in the kitchen?"

Kara opted for the kitchen, even choosing to dress first in her denim overalls that Rita had so kindly washed. With Hannah assisting her, she felt ready to meet the rest of the family. Martin greeted

Kara with a genuine embrace of love, expressing his joy in her salvation. He offered to relieve Hannah and to help Kara to the kitchen. Kara flushed with pleasure at the older man's affection. It had been years since she had had a father's hug and love expressed that way.

Kara finished her soup and was ready to explain what lead to her salvation experience when Cody entered the kitchen. She had noticed he was not with the rest of the family and had assumed he was working somewhere on the ranch. Sincerely delighted to see him, she was eager to share her testimony, her face beaming and her eyes coming alive with excitement.

Rita and Hannah wanted to know all the details from start to finish concerning the dream she had had. The family listened, sitting on the edges of their seats as Kara described the dream. The women cried all over again by the end of the story. The men were deeply moved as well. Cody was quick to notice that Kara's emphasis was more on Jesus in the dream than on Jonny. He was beginning to feel hopeful; maybe there was a possibility that he and Kara could have a future together. Maybe it was a slim chance, but hope was what he had, if only a meager amount. Back at the pond, after he had dried his tears, he had sat a while longer, waiting for the peace of God. Once again he let go of Kara, very much aware of the fact that his love for her seemed to grow instead of diminish. If only by the grace of God she could belong to him! He would wait.

The telephone rang. Davey had called faithfully every day to check up on his sister. Rita wore a broad smile as she gave the telephone to Kara, understanding her desire to share the good news with her brother. He was certain to be as excited as anyone to know of his sister's conversion.

Kara told her brother of her experience and how it had all come about. The entire Ralston family could hear the whoop and holler on the other end of the line as Davey expressed his joy. He had been more burdened for his sister than anyone. Davey asked when she thought she could come home. Kara assured him that the day after tomorrow should be fine. Rita frowned, not totally prepared to give up her young, pregnant charge. Davey then cut the conversation short, eager to call Bobbie with the news.

... All Things Become New ...

    Kara and the Ralstons spent time reading and discussing the Word. The Scriptures seemed to come alive for Kara. There was so much to learn, so many questions she wanted to ask. Martin smiled with understanding, assuring Kara that there was always tomorrow or the next day. Everyone, especially Kara, needed rest. A blanket of peace and contentment rested on the entire household as they retired to their rooms.

    For once, Kara no longer felt the need to reach across the bed to the emptiness. She knew that she would someday see Jonny again.

. . . 22

AFTER RETURNING HOME, KARA WAS HERSELF AGAIN IN A FEW DAYS. Time passed quickly with her busy schedule. Davey fretted that she was doing too much, admonishing her to slow down, if only for his sake. She was driving him to distraction with her busyness! Flustered, he sometimes threatened to lock her in her bedroom for a few days. Kara only laughed, giving her brother a brief hug as she went merrily on her way. She liked being busy, although the weight of the baby was beginning to feel cumbersome.

Sandy lent a sympathetic and understanding ear whenever Kara explained how she was feeling about the pregnancy and her growing abdomen. Her midwife, Joyce Andrews, was pleased with Kara's health at each visit Joyce made to the house. In her sixth month of pregnancy, what would have been her seventh wedding anniversary came around. It was a Sunday, and although she had been attending church with Davey, she felt she needed time alone. Davey understood and respectfully agreed to attend church alone, if she thought she would be OK. Kara promised she would be fine.

A month had passed since her dream and conversion. Kara had grown so much spiritually in that short time. Reading Jonny's Bible had become a necessity in her life, something she did before beginning her day. Hannah had encouraged her to make a habit of it, guaranteeing the results would be worth the effort. Hannah had been right.

Kara nestled as well as she could into the chair beside her bedroom window, giving her growing stomach a gentle love pat. "You're taking up more space all the time. You know that don't you?" she said, with a rueful grin. As if in reply, the baby gave a sharp kick to the ribs. As she was in the habit of doing, Kara wrapped her arms around her stomach as if to hold the little one.

She could not help but think of Jonny. This would have been their special day together, like the six others before it—just the two of them. They had thought they would grow old together. She had cried so many tears. Oddly, she honestly did not feel like crying. The idea of her husband being gone was sad, but since she had accepted Christ into her heart, with the promise of eternal life, she had a peace. She knew it was OK to grieve, but she did not feel the hopelessness that she had felt before. Jesus Christ was her hope! Unconsciously, she toyed with the wedding band on her finger once again. Somehow, it did not seem right that she should take it off this particular day.

The Psalms had become dear to her heart in her young walk with the Lord. They continued to be the healing balm she needed on her wounded, grieving heart, but today she happened to open the Bible to Isaiah 40:11: "He tends his flock like a shepherd: He gathers the lambs in his arms and carries them close to his heart; He gently leads those that have young." She felt the presence of the Holy Spirit as she read the words.

The Scripture spoke volumes of the love of God for her and the baby she carried. She was certain that the believers were praying for her during the church service. She could feel the love of God envelope her. Placing the Bible on the small table beside the chair, Kara closed her eyes to surrender to that love, absorbing it like a dry sponge. It's no wonder Jonny had been so excited and animated after his salvation. Even her brother had been elated and had wanted to share. Whom should she share with?

A sudden thought startled Kara. She had never told her inlaws of her salvation. She remembered how Jonny had tried to tell them about his conversion, but no one had listened. How would they respond to her news? She boldly dialed the phone number.

Jaime Madison answered the telephone for his parents. He was surprised and pleased to hear her voice. All the Madisons had been thinking especially about her and Jonny today, wondering how she was doing. Kara assured him that she was fine. Jaime knew it was probably bad timing, but he had been feeling pressed for quite a while to reach a decision concerning where he and his new bride would live. His mortgage loan had been approved. All that remained was for him to find a house in the price range the bank allowed. Would she consider selling her house to him?

The timing indeed seemed wrong. Kara was prepared to sell to her brother-in-law, but she felt slightly exasperated at getting sidetracked from the reason for her call. She decided not to get upset and fight it. Soon they were in deep conversation about details. The price he offered for the house was reasonable enough. She agreed to arrive early for his wedding to sign the legal papers and to go through the house, choosing what she did or did not want. That gave her one week to prepare to leave, which seemed too soon. Her mind spun with all the matters she needed to attend to before then.

"Come back to earth, Kara," Jaime said. "I'm sure you want to talk to mom and dad. Hold on."

Jonathan and Alice got on the speakerphone. Kara thought it was good to hear their voices. They explained that they had kept in touch with the Ralstons. Kara found it interesting that her in-laws seemed to know more about what was going on in Montana than she did.

"We're certainly looking forward to seeing you again, dear," Alice stated with sincerity.

"Jaime and I have agreed on a price for the house, which means I'm going to have to come a week early to work out the legal matters pertaining to the property and to deal with the contents."

Kara would give them the necessary details regarding her flight number and time of arrival when she knew more. Jonathan was hesitant to broach the subject of Jonny, sensitive as to whether or not Kara wanted to talk about him. Much to his relief, Kara assured him she was doing well despite this particular day being their anniversary date and the fact that it was supposed to be a day of celebration. Once again, the timing did not seem right to talk about the Lord and her recent experience. That would have to wait until she was able to visit with the couple personally. There was a moment of silence on the line as both Jonathan and Alice became too emotional to speak.

"Well, Kara, I must say that you do sound happy, just as you did when we were out there. I'm glad you're doing so well. I guess I'm getting old and sentimental, while you're young and ready to go on with life."

"I don't know about that, Alice. If I consider this baby I'm carrying—the thought of losing him or her is nearly unbearable. I can't imagine the loss of a grown son. I guess we need to dwell on the good memories we have."

"That's a positive outlook," Jonathan said with a heavy sigh. "It seems with the passing of time, it gets more difficult instead of easier."

Not sure if it was the proper timing to discuss the Lord, Kara chose the easy way out. "We'll have some time to visit and talk when I get there, OK?"

The conversation ended on a sad note of sorts. Kara felt the best thing she could do for her in-laws was to pray. She became burdened for her loved ones and spent some time praying for those dear to her heart.

Davey arrived home at a decent hour, desiring to spend time with his sister. The two had a quiet lunch, Kara sharing her concern for the Madisons with Davey. He mentioned he had been praying for the family and would continue to do so.

The remainder of the day passed uneventfully as the two took a walk and then watched a John Wayne video, much to Davey's delight. They chose to make an early evening of it and were in bed before 9:30 P.M.

✢   ✢   ✢

Kara and Davey made arrangements for Kara to take two weeks off from work, giving her plenty of time to visit the Madisons and to tie up loose ends concerning the belongings in her house. Sandy and another woman were able to fill in for Kara. Before she knew it, it was time for her departure. Too busy with last-minute details, she hadn't had time to visit with the Ralston family, much to her disappointment.

Davey took her to the airport to see her off. The in-laws were there to greet her at the other end. Kara could not help but notice the damp chill to the air.

The elder Madisons exclaimed over and over about how well she looked in her seventh month of pregnancy. She admitted to having cheated somewhat at the airport in the Midwest. Since Kara had had such little time to change planes, the gentleman with the cart to transport passengers between terminals and gates had had compassion on her. She had been relieved that he was willing to come to her rescue. The three had a good laugh with Kara following her confession.

Outside, she noticed the leaves were in the early stages of autumn colors. Kara secretly hoped she would see the leaves when they were at their peak in beautiful colors of red, yellow, and gold.

"This is a perfect time for a wedding," she told Jonathan and Alice.

Arriving at the Madisons' house, Alice suggested Kara should freshen up and maybe get some rest before dinner. Jaime and Jason, who would be along at dinner time, were most eager to see her. To Kara, a rest sounded delightful after her hectic schedule of preparations to leave Montana. Kara retired to Jason's room. He had given up his room to her and would sleep on the hide-a-bed in the living room.

As she settled into bed, Kara had to admit she was tired. She had not slept well the night before in her excitement over the coming trip. Her mind whirled with all the duties she had to attend to while back east, mentally checking off a list while the clock ticked on.

✤ ✤ ✤

A rested Kara entered the kitchen to the smell of roasted chicken. The delightful aroma stirred her hunger. She was ready to eat if no one else was!

The entire Madison family, as well as Jaime's fiancée, were present to greet her. Kara took an immediate liking to Ann, certain she was a wonderful match for her brother-in-law. Everyone exchanged greetings and hugs, the family delighting in the healthy picture Kara portrayed. Everyone expressed the fact that Montana appeared to agree with her.

Kara could not refute that. Only two months to go and then she would have the little one in her arms! Talk reverted to the coming wedding and Kara's house, Jaime questioning if she was up to going to the place to deal with everything.

Kara answered with an appreciative smile. "Yes, I honestly am, Jaime. In fact, I plan to go tomorrow and look the situation over and see what needs to be done."

The entire family cast understanding looks her way, marveling at the strength of the young woman and the fact that she could state her plans so matter-of-factly, none of them desiring to be in her shoes.

Ann's blue eyes lit up with pleasure as she spoke, breaking the silence. "Kara, you have such wonderful taste in furniture! I love your choice of colors too."

Kara thanked her for the compliment as Ann continued to share some ideas of her own about changes she would like to make. It was not a problem at all for Kara to offer help in any way she could. Ann appreciated the offer, feeling slightly overwhelmed with the coming wedding and all there was to do. Kara suggested she shouldn't worry about the house too much the way it was and she should see it as a challenge after the wedding. Ann agreed that that approach would be best and not so stressful.

The evening together went fast for all the Madisons. Jaime left the house to take Ann home, while the remaining Madisons did some more catching up on news and people they had met while in Montana. Before they realized, it was time to retire for the evening. Everyone had plenty to do tomorrow.

✤ ✤ ✤

Jason loaned Kara his sports car while she was visiting. She felt honored that he was willing to part with the little gem, although she was not sure she fit the role, being pregnant and all. It was a bit trying to maneuver around the steering wheel and to get in and out of the vehicle. She hated to complain, but the car was totally impractical for her round figure. Maybe she would rent a car. She missed Davey's light pickup.

Kara found herself at the front door of her home before she wanted to be. She had thought she would be mentally prepared for this, but it was not as easy as she had thought. There were nearly seven years of memories beyond the door, and she knew there was no Jonny on the other side waiting for her. Hesitantly, she unlocked the door. The house was dark and empty, having a musty odor to it. Kara opened the shades and windows to allow the fresh, crisp October air to circulate through the house. Everything appeared to be as she had left it. Pictures still hung on the walls and clothes still hung in the closet. She felt removed from it all, as though it belonged to someone else in another time and place.

Jaime had been kind enough to collect empty boxes for her to fill. He had offered to take the day off from work to help her. No one had wanted her go alone to the house that first time, yet she felt it was something she had to do herself. She was unsure how she would react, and she really wanted to be alone with her thoughts. How does one pack away over six years of memories? Jaime and Ann had made it easy for her. They had suggested she take what she wanted and leave the rest. They would choose the items they were interested in, pay for them, and would sell or give away the rest.

Kara decided to begin in her bedroom, tackling the closets and dressers first. It troubled her to see Jonny's clothes and all the familiar items that were his. Since the Madison men were similar in size, Kara thought they should have first choice of the clothes. That would make her job easier too. Sorting through her late husband's closet and dresser drawers, Kara did not find anything she particularly wanted to keep, except for his coin collection, which she thought their child would appreciate when he, or she was older. She had Jonny's Bible and somehow that was enough. A few clothes she had left behind were next. She wondered if anything would fit once the baby was born. Well, she could hope for the best. She chose some favorites and put the remainder into boxes to go to the Salvation Army. The list went on and on with the duties that needed to be dealt with.

Kara was so engrossed, she never heard Alice calling for her. Her mother-in-law had brought lunch as she had said she would. The Madisons were concerned about leaving Kara alone too long in the house for fear she would become too upset. It was obvious to Alice that Kara had indeed been busy, much to her relief. She encouraged her daughter-in-law to take time to relax and eat something, fussing that she had best not overdo. Kara gave Alice a warm smile and thanked her for her concern, promising not to exhaust herself.

Alice had the afternoon free to help Kara in any way she could. As the two worked, they talked of Jonny and this or that in the house that prompted a memory. It was a time of healing for both of them. Alice could not help but notice the peace and calmness Kara had as they worked. She herself had dreaded entering the house and remembering her son, but somehow Kara's acceptance of the situation comforted her as well. Alice felt better about being there than she had thought possible. Before the women knew it, it was time to quit for dinner. They were to meet Jon and Jason at a restaurant in town, which suited them fine, as both were too exhausted to think of cooking.

The dinner was pleasant. Jon was concerned that Kara could be overdoing it, suggesting she should stay longer if need be. Kara assured him that she was fine, although she did admit to feeling tired. If she needed more time, it was not a big deal. Davey had raised his eyebrows at the mention of staying two weeks, advising her to take more time if necessary and not to worry about anything there.

✣   ✣   ✣

The week flew by, with Kara taking advantage of any help offered her. The sorting had to come to a halt due to the wedding. Ann was a delightful person to be around and gratefully accepted any suggestions Kara offered. Being a friend of Bobbie Brooks had its rewards. Kara assisted Ann in decorating the interior of the church pews with cream-colored bows and baby's-breath. She created a simple centerpiece of autumn leaves and white candles. All the while, Kara talked much of her friends in Montana, creating a desire in her family to visit sometime.

The wedding uniting Jaime and Ann was beautiful, making memories for the two in the years to come. Kara was confident they would be very happy, hoping and praying they would have many years ahead. The ceremony brought back a few precious memories of her own, and she felt thankful for the years she and

. . . Audrey Marr . . .

Jonny had had together. Kara was feeling special and rather elegant this day. Her in-laws had insisted on buying the dress she wore. It was a dark mauve color with short sleeves and a rounded neckline. Her light brown hair was simply brushed away from her face to cascade midway down her back.

Kara felt many curious, as well as sympathetic, eyes upon her. It was not a huge city she had lived in, but because of Jonny's vocation as a car salesman, he dealt with a lot of the public. She was sure her presence aroused conversation among quite a few people.

During the wedding reception, Jaime asked Kara to dance with him following the usual bride and groom's first dance as Mr. and Mrs. Kara was caught off guard with this request, especially being pregnant. She was grateful for the slow music and for the flat shoes she wore.

As the two began dancing among the throng, Kara gave her brother-in-law a tender smile. She knew Jaime and Jonny had been close brothers. "It was a lovely wedding, Jaime. I'm certain you and Ann will have many happy years together."

"I'm planning on it," he stated with a smile. He suddenly sobered. "I know a wedding is supposed to be a happy time, but I can't help thinking of Jon and wishing he were here. I have to admit I miss him a great deal. He was a great brother. We had a lot of fun times together."

Kara nodded her head. She wanted to share with her brother-in-law about Jesus Christ and what He had done for her, but it did not seem an appropriate time. Weddings were supposed to be happy, joyous celebrations, not times for sentimental tears or serious talk. For an unexplained reason, she felt it was all right to wait. The moment for sharing from her heart would come.

Jonathan Madison claimed Kara for the next slow dance, complimenting her on her lovely appearance and the healthy glow to her face. The two chatted amiably until the music stopped and they parted.

Standing to the side while observing the celebration and people about her, a male voice spoke from behind. "Hello, Kara."

At the mention of her name, Kara turned to acknowledge the speaker. "Tim, this is a surprise! How are you?"

"I'm fine. You're looking great considering everything you've been through the past several months."

Tim Werner was a fellow classmate of Kara and Jonny's from high school. Through the years, he and Jonny had shared the same interests: boating and fishing. His congenial personality made up for the slightly crooked teeth and long nose on a long, narrow face. Boating was the one interest Kara had not shared with Jonny. The thought of deep water just below her always made her feel queasy and frightened. She liked her feet firmly planted on the ground! Her husband had been forced to find a fishing partner. It was a carry-over from high school days. Being present at the time of the boating accident, Tim had felt responsible, in no small degree, for the death of his friend. Seeing Kara with child brought back painful memories. He knew Jonny had always wanted children, a half-dozen if he could have gotten Kara to agree to it.

"Oh, Tim, you've always been a compassionate person. Are you really OK?"

With a helpless shrug of his shoulders, Tim was at a loss for words. Kara studied him as he looked toward the floor of dancers to hide the emotions flooding him.

"Let's get some punch and sit down somewhere, Tim."

With refreshments in their hands, the two found a place away from most of the crowd.

"Jaime and Ann make a nice couple, don't they?" Tim asked, as he looked once again at the people on the dance floor, the bride and groom among them, and refusing to look directly at Kara.

"I'm under the impression you're afraid to look at me, Tim. What is it?"

"I'm sorry, Kara," he said, as he reluctantly turned to look directly at her. "You do look great. Actually, you look better than I had expected. The Madisons said you were going to be here today."

"What? You think I should be some shriveled up widow always wringing my hands and crying?" Her light attempt at humor failed.

"No, no! Nothing like that." Tim shrugged his shoulders again. "Do you think you would like to sell Jonny's share of the boat to me? Being half-owner with you doesn't seem right somehow."

"Sure," Kara replied with a gentle smile. "I know Jonny would've wanted that."

Tilting his head to really look at Kara, he studied her for a moment. "There's something different about you, Kara. You seem happy, and—I don't know—at peace? What is it?"

Kara's face lit with excitement. Finally, here was someone she could share her testimony with. "Several weeks ago I accepted Christ, who now lives in my heart. It was a long time coming, but it was clearly one of the best decisions I have ever made."

Tim squirmed in his discomfort. Here it was again! Jonny had made this very statement to him only a week before his death. If Jesus were so special, then why did such a tragedy come about to affect both Jonny and Kara for all time?

Kara could see the wall immediately rise between them as Tim stiffened following her confession. Uncertain how much she should say, Kara was not to be easily discouraged. "Jonny tried to share his experience with me, but I didn't want to hear any of it. I was so cold toward him. It wasn't until months later that I realized that I, like Jonny, did need Jesus. Davey and others in Montana have been so supportive and loving—long before I became a Christian. I think that was one reason why I saw my need. I had never before understood the love God had for me to give His only son, Jesus, who was willing to be a living sacrifice for everyone. He died for you, Tim!"

With a wry grin, Tim reacted negatively to all she said. He did not want to hear this stuff. "Can we change the subject?"

"Sure. No problem."

Conversation turned to happenings in town and people they knew. Time passed quickly for the two. Before they realized it, it was time for the bride and groom to depart. After goodbyes were said, the guests took their leave and the immediate family was left to tidy the reception room. Tim offered his help and asked if he could escort Kara to the Madisons' house. Somewhat surprised by the request, the young widow accepted the ride.

On the way and not certain when she would see him again, Kara asked Tim if he would like any of Jonny's fishing equipment. Tim was pleased with the idea and said as much. Kara suggested they go to her house and get the items, deciding it was easier to take care of the matter now when she had the time.

Tim had driven countless times to Jonny's place following his death, to sit and stare for long periods of time at the abandoned house and all the changes within. When would the guilt and weight of it all dissolve? Kara had no idea how difficult it was for him to think of going into the house where Jonny had lived so happily. His friend was too young to have been robbed of life. Anger replaced the guilt as he thought about the young widow sitting next to him, expecting a child that Jonny should have been allowed to be a father to. Life wasn't fair. Nothing was fair.

Retrieving the keys from her purse, Kara unlocked the garage door and flipped a switch to illuminate the inside of the building. Kara directed Tim to the fishing gear and a few other items she thought he would be interested in. Owning something of Jonny's was a connection of sorts, easing some of the frustration he felt. Tim was able to fit the articles in the trunk of his car. He noticed Kara was quiet on the way to the Madisons' house, saying little.

"Are you all right, Kara?" he asked with concern.

"Yes. I'm sorry, Tim. I guess I'm feeling the effects of such a busy day. Right now I feel as if I could sleep for a week."

"I thought you said you were told to take it easy. Was today difficult? What I mean is, did it stir a lot of painful memories?"

"To tell the truth, it made me thankful for the memories I do have. Jonny and I wanted to grow old together, but the Lord is sovereign and knows best. I guess He thought Jonny was needed in Heaven. We don't always understand God's ways. He says in Isaiah 55:8–9 that we don't think or do things the way God does. His ways are higher than ours. Just this morning I read those verses. I'm glad I did. It kind of helps a person understand things better to keep a clear perspective. I realize I don't have to have all the answers to life's questions. It's enough knowing I have the Lord and He is enough."

"That's certainly a positive perspective."

"But you can have this same Lord and Savior, Tim."

"I'll think about it, Kara."

Knowing she had to be satisfied with his answer, Kara prayed he would.

Seeing Kara safely to the door, Tim declined the invitation to come in, mentioning the hour was already late. He did ask concerning her plans for the morrow. When she told him she was going with Jon and Alice to the house, Tim asked if he could help in

... Audrey Marr ...

some way. Kara was touched by his willingness and gratefully accepted his offer, expressing the need for any able and willing person. They agreed to rendezvous at nine o'clock.

The Madisons had waited for Kara's return to be certain all was well. Everyone was thankful to call it a day.

✣   ✣   ✣

Following the day of the wedding, Tim was at Kara's house every spare moment to assist her as much as he was able. Kara was beginning to wonder if he had any kind of social life, or if he even ate a hot meal. Of course, he was a bachelor, she reasoned, and she was grateful for the help. Since she could not do heavy lifting of any kind, she appreciated Tim's strong back and told him so. His reply was that he was more than glad to help in any way he could.

It dawned on Kara after a few days that Tim's efforts were based on guilt. She prayed often for her friend throughout the day. Having to deal with her own grief, she had not considered what Tim was going through these past months. Uncertain as to how to broach the subject, Kara offered to treat Tim to dinner one evening, hoping to draw out her friend. Tim was reluctant to accept, but Kara was adamant.

Kara felt a steak dinner was in order, insisting she could not have gotten as much done had he not helped. The Madisons had been so busy with the wedding and family-owned business that they had not been as much help to Kara as they would have liked. Both Jon and Alice had been grateful for Tim's offer to help, feeling guilty themselves for not being able to do more for their daughter-in-law. They did feel better knowing she seemed to be dealing with things just fine. There did not seem to be enough of them to go around. As it was, Kara was going to be able to leave the day after next, as planned. She was missing Davey and her friends in Montana. She marveled at how much she had come to accept Montana as home, not missing friends in town at all. There hadn't seemed to be time for friends or a social life with so much to do.

Seated in a somewhat private place in the restaurant, their orders placed, Kara and Tim made small talk about his work as a carpenter. He had a few building projects going on that interested Kara. The two felt comfortable with one another, being old friends.

When the conversation lagged and dinner was nearly finished, Kara expressed her appreciation for all the assistance Tim had given her.

Tim was quick to shrug it off as a small matter. "I really wish there were more I could do for you. If there ever is, you let me know, Kara, OK?"

"Thank you, Tim." Kara looked into his brown eyes as she launched into deeper discussion. "You don't feel guilty and blame yourself for what happened to Jonny, do you?"

Tim couldn't hold her gaze. "No, of course not."

Kara looked at him skeptically to let him know he was not fooling her.

Uncomfortable with the steady, green eyes, he blurted out, "OK, I admit to feeling some guilt." He felt flustered that she had been able to extract a confession from him. "There isn't a day that goes by that I don't wonder if there weren't something I could've done to have saved Jonny. I've played it all over and over in my mind, trying to figure out what went wrong. It all happened so fast! Jonny was over the side of the boat and had seemingly disappeared."

"Yes, and if I remember correctly, the police called it what it was—an accident. You have your whole life ahead of you, Tim. Please don't waste the years with guilt. Jonny wouldn't want it that way, nor do I. Life is too short."

Tim was deeply moved by Kara's words as she continued. "You know, I too lived with guilt after Jonny died. He had tried to tell me about Jesus, and I felt that it was some religious fling he was having and that it would pass. I was cool toward him many times. Then as the weeks passed following Jonny's death, I pondered the things he had said to me and reflected on my own actions. Then Jesus came along in the form of my brother and friends. It was their love and the Lord dealing with my hard heart. I had no peace. I was like a person being tossed about on the high, rough waves of life, desperately trying to make sense of everything. And then to have a baby on top of everything else! I feel so blessed now. The Lord is good and He loves you and me so much more than we could ever love anyone. The Bible explains how the Lord forgives and remembers our sins no more. His mercies and grace are great towards us."

Tim could not refute the young widow. He could see she was sincere, her face beaming and eyes sparkling. Maybe what she said was true and worth considering. Smiling, he thanked Kara for her honesty. Kara was pleased with his response and suggested they have dessert. As the two continued to enjoy light conversation, Kara noticed a few people she knew and thought gossip was sure to spread around town after tonight. There was no way she would mention this to Tim, who seemed the most relaxed he had been all evening.

Kara was glad for her bed that night, glad to know that in less than two days she would be in Montana again. With a contented sigh, she snuggled under the covers and was soon fast asleep.

✣ ✣ ✣

Kara was concerned that she had not been able to share her testimony with her in-laws. The day before her departure, after spending time in the Word, she prayed the Lord would help her to be a witness to her family. The opportunity came that evening as everyone sat around the dinner table following a delicious meal Kara had insisted on preparing. The family was reminded that Kara would be leaving on the morrow; time was a precious commodity. The subject of the house and Jonny surfaced after some time. Kara decided it was a good time to share with the Madisons the story of her salvation and how it all had come about. She asked if they remembered how Jonny had come to all of them, excited about his salvation experience.

Yes, they clearly remembered the day.

"I have to confess that I didn't care to hear Jonny out," Kara said. "I thought it was something that would pass with time, but he only seemed to become more excited about accepting Jesus as his Savior. Alice, you mentioned to me that with time Jonny's death wasn't getting easier with you."

Alice responded with a nod, curious as to where this was leading.

"While in Montana sorting through my feelings of loss and pain, Davey was so kind and loving to me. I made other friends, most of whom you met while in Montana. It took some time, but I came to the realization that I needed Jesus. He was only waiting for me to turn to Him. The peace I have found is beyond any words, but I am content in the Lord." She wanted to tell of the dream she had, but she felt she had already said enough, noticing the three Madisons squirming in their seats.

Jonathan spoke while studying his hands, as though he hoped to read something there. "I don't understand all of what you're saying, but I've often thought of how cool I was toward J.J. when he approached me. I didn't care to hear about religion. It makes me feel bad when I look back on the way I treated my son."

Kara hadn't heard Jonny's nickname since his death—a name the family had given him since he was the second Jonathan in the family. She knew what it was like to go through the grieving process without the Lord, and she ached for these dear ones. "Would you please consider what I've told you all this evening?" she asked gently. "And feel free to call me anytime if you would like to hear more. I'm sure Davey is more qualified than I about spiritual matters, but I'll do my best."

Looking first to her husband for his silent approval, Alice cast her daughter-in-law a weak smile with a nod of her head before changing the subject.

The remainder of the evening passed quickly for all of them.

...23

DAVEY WAS WAITING FOR HIS SISTER AT THE GATE WHEN SHE DISEMBARKED from the plane. Goodbyes had been difficult, but knowing her brother was waiting at the end of her journey helped ease the parting. It had been a pleasant flight, but Kara was delighted to be home. *Yes*, she suddenly realized, *Montana is home.*

There would be so much catching up to do with her friends, but that would have to come later. She wanted quality time with her brother so they could talk of the many changes back east. *My, he looks handsome*, she thought as he greeted her with a hearty hug, exclaiming that she had definitely grown since he had seen her last. Kara rewarded him with a light punch on his arm before walking away to claim her baggage.

The drive to Davey's house reminded Kara of the first time she had stepped foot in Montana. My, how much she had changed the past six months or so, and for the better she hoped. Here she was—pregnant, yet no longer grieving and hurting as she had in the beginning. Yes, it was like coming home.

As they entered the house, the pleasing aroma of her favorite dish came wafting toward her nostrils. Turning to her brother, she smiled in delight. "I suppose Bobbie had a part in what my nose is telling me is lasagna?"

Davey rewarded her comment with a broad grin of his own. "Yep. She insisted on welcoming you home with a hearty dish that she knew would please you."

"Davey, I don't know of anything she can't cook well. You had better take hold of that girl and not lose her!"

In her excitement of being home, Kara did not notice the dark shadow that passed over her brother's face. Davey was glad he was not expected to reply. His relationship with Bobbie was suddenly going nowhere, leaving him confused and frustrated. Bobbie herself was very evasive.

Kara offered to put dinner on the table while Davey took her luggage to the bedroom. Before long the two were feeling satisfied with their stomachs full of the delicious food—lasagna, green salad, and fresh rolls. Following clean up, the two settled in the living room to continue to catch up on news back home. Kara mentioned to her brother that she expected boxes of furniture to arrive any day, having shipped them only yesterday. There were some pieces that had belonged to her grandmother and mother, which she had wanted to keep.

Davey suggested for her sake they retire about ten o'clock. Kara was happy to comply.

✢   ✢   ✢

Kara was in full swing a few days after arriving in Montana. She felt as though she had been gone forever, especially after seeing Emily Rose again. My how that baby had grown! She was able to sit up with pillows around her, and she had become such a busy little girl. It made Kara impatient to have her own baby in her arms. Sandy assured Kara that the time would pass quickly and the baby would be born before she was ready for it.

Kara made it a point to return Bobbie's dishes as soon as she could. There was so much catching up to do. Bobbie had been too busy preparing for an upcoming wedding to make it out to Dave's house. She had finished the floral arrangements and other decorations just that morning and was delighted to see Kara enter the floral shop. Bobbie's mother, Peg, insisted the two go out to lunch and allow her to operate the shop.

... Audrey Marr ...

The women chose a small café around the corner from the floral shop. After they had ordered, Bobbie turned to Kara, her blue eyes huge with excitement. "I missed you, Kara! I'm so glad you're back." She leaned forward in her seat, anxious to talk. "I want to hear everything about your visit with family, especially details of the wedding."

Kara smiled at Bobbie's enthusiasm. "I'm so glad I have you for a friend! You were a lifesaver for sharing ideas with me about flower arrangements. I was able to help decorate the church and reception area for Jaime and Ann. She chose cream and cranberry colors for the decorations. We made bows out of crepe paper for the church pews and a floral arrangement for the front of the church. The bridesmaids wore beautiful, stylish gowns of cranberry color. They looked so pretty! As it was, everything was a success, and the newlyweds are delighted with my house."

Time passed quickly for the two as they visited. Bobbie glanced at her watch and decided she had better return to the shop to give her mom a break. Kara had to get home and prepare dinner. It was Wednesday and she was putting forth a special effort to be present at Bible study that evening.

The Bible study group was excited to see Kara again and to see her looking so well. They greeted her with warm embraces. Kara had an insatiable hunger to hear the Word. It was wonderful to hear Dennis teaching from the Scriptures. There was so much Kara felt she needed to learn; if she weren't careful she could get overwhelmed.

Kara was able to mix and mingle with most everyone after refreshments were served. She was disappointed that neither Cody nor Hannah were present, yet she was interested to hear the announcement about a harvest potluck and hayride at the Ralston ranch two Saturdays from then.

On the way home, Kara asked Davey, "Have you seen any of the Ralston family?"

"You've got to be kidding me!" Davey quipped, grinning. "When do you think I had time for a social life while you were away? I was too busy working, doing my own laundry, and cooking!"

"I can see that all I'm good for is being your personal maid!" Kara said dryly, rolling her eyes.

Davey laughed as he gave his sister a gentle squeeze on the shoulder. "I'm just kidding, Kar. I promise it's not true, although I am more than happy to have you back."

Kara gave her brother's hand a light pat as she cast him a loving smile. He meant more to her than words could say.

Bedtime was not long in coming. As Kara snuggled under the cozy blankets, she felt quite content and at peace with her world. She found the most comfortable position was on one side or the other now. The baby was definitely growing and active. Anymore, when she chose to lie quiet and sleep, the baby was awake, kicking and moving around. She was hoping when the little one was born that it would be less active. Wrapping her arms around her abdomen, she slept.

✣   ✣   ✣

Since her return to Montana, Tim Werner had called occasionally to chat with Kara. It did his heart and Kara's good to be able to converse after so many months of silence. Aware that Kara did not blame him for Jonny's death had eased a great deal of the guilt he bore. As Kara shared scriptures she had read or something new she had learned, attempting to encourage her friend, Tim discovered he looked forward to hearing more of what she had to say. He had purchased a Bible shortly after Kara had returned to Montana so he could read for himself what Kara had told him. With the help of the index, he was able to find books of the Bible Kara had spoken of and read. Soon he was in Genesis reading of creation, the tower of Babel, and so many other stories. In the evenings when his busy day was over, Tim had his nose in the Bible. It was as though he could not get enough of it, the pages and stories coming alive for the young man.

Kara noted changes taking place in Tim's heart, an action she would have never dreamed of. During their conversations, he would share what he had been reading about. She could tell by the tone of his voice he was getting excited. Sometimes she wanted to shout and rejoice from the rooftops at recognizing her friend's spiritual journey and progress. He no longer had to feel guilty about the past, and he was closer to accepting the love and forgiveness of God than even he realized.

Nearly two weeks after her return to Montana, Kara had an afternoon to herself. As she sat in the chair by her bedroom window, she read the Bible. Closing the book, she meditated on what she had read and on the goodness of the Lord. Kara's eyes wandered to her wedding band. She thought of how far Tim had come in his search for the Lord, satisfied with the changes and happenings in her life, as well as the others. Jonny would have been so happy for her and Tim. She looked again at her wedding band and was not sure she was ready to part with it yet feeling confident that she would know when the time was right.

✤   ✤   ✤

It was Saturday, the day of the hayride. Kara had decided to make barbecued meatballs and a lemon cake for the potluck. She was anxious to see her gelding, Rebel, and to know how he was doing. Before leaving for the east, she had encouraged the Ralstons to ride him, aware of the fact that she was only going to get bigger in the days ahead. But most of all, she was eager to visit the Ralston family and to know how they had fared the past month. She had sorely missed all of them.

It was a near-perfect October day for the outing. The sun felt warm with the air a little crisp. Davey had them to the Lazy R Ranch in no time. A number of people from Bible study were already present. Kara wondered if she should venture into the house for a chat with Rita or Hannah but thought better of it with so many others to talk to.

The dishes of food were placed on a long table. Rita came out of the house, her hands full of plates and napkins. Once she had placed the articles on the table, she approached Kara. It was clear the older woman was pleased to see her.

"I'm so glad you could make it today, Kara!" Rita said as she gave her a warm hug. "As hostess, I've got a lot to do before the food is served, but I promise that we'll talk later, all right?"

"I understand, Rita. Is there anything I can do to help?"

"Not really, Dear, but thank you for offering. There are already several women who have volunteered to help me. You just make yourself comfortable in a chair and relax."

With those words, Rita quickly ushered the volunteers into the house to help where needed.

Drew and Sandy were among the last of the families to arrive. Bobbie was not feeling well and had decided to stay home. It wasn't long before Dennis asked the blessing over the food and the evening and folks were lined up with paper plates in hand to partake of the food. While people were helping themselves to the food, Kara sought out Rita for a chat.

Rita was more than happy to oblige her.

"My, Kara, you have blossomed in the past month or so. You certainly are a picture of health. I can see the Lord in you as well. Your face is glowing and it's obvious to anyone that you have a profound peace."

Kara smiled at the compliment concerning her walk with the Lord, before wrinkling her nose. "You're so sweet, Rita! I'm glad to know you see Christ in me, but as far as my figure—I keep telling myself that I don't look as big as I feel."

"Oh, nonsense, you look wonderful!" Rita comforted her with a light pat on the arm. "Oh, I'm supposed to tell you that Hannah regretted not being here. Before she knew the date set for the hayride, she had made a prior commitment to assist with a promotional for the upcoming winter fair. Planning begins early for such events. She told me to relay a message to you and to tell you that as soon as she can, she'll have a long, desired chat with you."

The two continued to visit for a few minutes longer before Rita excused herself to attend to minor details as hostess. She encouraged Kara to get in line while the food was hot and there was lots of it, promising to visit with her again later.

Kara dawdled a while until the line diminished and she was free to help herself. Davey and the Toomeys had already been served and asked her to sit with them. There were so many delicious foods; Kara had a difficult time choosing. After all, her plate was only so big! While trying to decide if she should take the ham or the chicken or both, a familiar voice spoke alongside her. "I'd take both if it were me. Mom made the chicken, and Mrs. Cooper always cooks a delicious ham."

"Cody, it's good to see you! It's been a while. How's Rebel doing?"

"Well," the rancher drawled, "it always makes a man feel special to have a woman ask about her horse before questioning him about his welfare."

Kara could feel the color rising from her neck to the roots of her hair. "Oh no, Cody!" she stammered. "I didn't mean that the way it sounded—honest."

Cody laughed, telling her she had gotten too serious in the past little while.

Kara liked to hear him laugh. As she looked at her friend, she was reminded again of what a pleasant face he had, his dark, blue eyes so warm. Realizing she was studying the man's face far too long, she quickly turned her attention to the dishes of food. None of this was lost on Cody. It pleased him to think she was showing some interest in him. He had done a lot of praying while she was gone. He had been worried that while among Jonny's family and her former friends, she might decide not to return to Montana.

Kara looked most attractive in her plaid shirt and jeans. She had tied her hair back with a red bandana, giving a western flair to her attire. Cody wanted to stare at her, to drink in the sight of her like the pure freshness of spring water. It was difficult to think of what he wanted to eat with the woman so close. He could have chosen sawdust for food and would have never noticed. She was wearing a light perfume that was causing him to feel heady with the aroma. He knew he was smitten with this woman—a goner was more like it.

They filled their plates quickly and found two lawn chairs. Conversation was merry among the friends. Drew held baby Emily as he tried to eat. The baby made several attempts to help herself to the plate of food with her hands. Not on solids yet, Emily was more curious than hungry, and she made great entertainment for the adults. When everyone had finished eating, Sandy gave Kara the baby to hold, promising her that there was plenty of help in the kitchen without either of them.

Kara could not argue. Cody thought she made quite a picture with the baby in her arms, her face animated and alive as she talked to her. It was obvious Emily was enjoying Kara as well, cooing in her excitement. Once again, Cody wondered what it would be like to be married to Kara. He wanted so much to protect her and the baby she was carrying. He had no problem at all raising someone else's baby, knowing he had been conceived in love and in a secure home. Cody was who he was and could not be anyone else. He felt good about that and was confident that with the Lord's help he would be able to do a fine job as a father. Well, maybe it scared him a little, having such a responsibility, but he had godly and positive footsteps to follow. He glanced over at his father and smiled.

Kara brought the rancher out of his deliberation by offering him the baby. His eyes were huge in disbelief that she would follow through with such an action. Babies were a problem in that he didn't know what to do with them or how to hold them.

Kara laughed. "Cody, I promise she won't break."

"Yeah, go ahead, Cody," Drew spoke up, attempting to encourage. "I wasn't sure what to do with Emily either. Besides, a man needs to learn that holding a baby is not something to be feared."

Reluctantly, Cody accepted the little girl, feeling quite awkward and uncertain as to what to do with her. Emily was used to being passed around and shared with others. She rewarded Cody with a toothless smile and coo, causing him to relax a bit as he held her on his lap.

"Look at that, Drew!" Davey stated good-naturedly. "I can see you're going to have to start early with that girl and keep her locked away for the next twenty-five years the way she bats those gorgeous, dark eyes of hers."

Drew chuckled. "You do have a point there, Dave. She has playing coy down pat."

While talk circulated around her, Kara noticed how well Cody did with the baby and thought he would make a great father. Emily, with her dark hair and complexion, could have been mistaken for his own. Flustered with the direction of her wandering thoughts, Kara decided to leave the men and find someone to visit with. Before she could move, Cody surrendered the baby to Drew, informing everyone he needed to help Martin hitch the team of draft horses for the hayride. Kara followed, scurrying to catch up as best she could in her condition.

Cody was both surprised and pleased to have her company.

"Could I see Rebel while the two of you hitch the team?" Kara asked, slightly breathless with hurrying.

Cody smiled at her obvious excitement. "Sure, he's right over there in the corral."

Martin smiled upon seeing Kara as he prepared to lead one of the draft horses from the corral. He gave her a firm hug. "Kara, it's so good to see you. You look as though motherhood agrees with you."

In the flurry and rush, he had not had time to visit or take note of who had come to the ranch. Kara returned the hug, blushing slightly with the older man's praise. She turned around to caress her gelding's neck, while the men hitched the team of horses. Rebel had stood patiently by, waiting for her attentions, enjoying her soft voice and touch. She loved the smell of horses and loved being around the animals. It would be wonderful to call a ranch such as this home, to be around such loving people. Sneaking a glance toward Cody, she wondered what he thought of her. Had he ever considered her anything more than a friend? Then again, she had given him no reason to think otherwise, what with her emotions on a roller coaster, the loss of Jonny and a baby on the way.

Everyone was soon aboard the flat wagon and on the road, with Martin handling the team. Kara was settled on a most comfortable bale of hay, which was covered with a blanket, near the front, where hopefully the bumps would not be too rough. Drew started a simple song and the others followed, his pleasant voice floating through the air. Emily was squirming in her excitement. She loved to hear her daddy sing. Kara was quite impressed hearing his voice. Sandy beamed with pride at her daughter and husband and reminded Kara that it was peculiar how the different twists in life could change everything. Sandy had been pregnant with Emily the last hayride and now Kara was expecting a baby. Who would have considered such a turn of events?

Cody did not want to be too obvious about his interest in Kara. He sat beside Davey and joined in the singing. There was too much noise to hear Kara sing, although he was aware she had a clear soprano voice, having heard her in Bible study and church.

Darkness had fallen by the time the wagon returned to the main house. Rita had stayed behind and started a bonfire. There was a definite chill to the air as everyone put on jackets and brought out the marshmallows and sticks. Cody took up his guitar, making certain Kara was in plain view. Dennis lead the group in prayer and then asked for song requests. Kara knew almost all the songs now, which greatly pleased her. She felt she had come a long way in the months since the last hayride. The singing was a delightful end to an evening of fun and fellowship. Families departed for home at a decent hour to be able to rise the next morning for church.

Noting Kara's disappointment at not being able to see Hannah, Davey asked the Ralstons if they would like to come to his house for a barbecue after church the next day. Everyone was delighted with the plan and resolved to keep things simple. Kara was thrilled with the idea of company, quickly putting together a menu, with the help of Rita.

... 24

The entire Ralston family attended church the following morning, although Cody came later, having to take care of a minor problem at the ranch. Apparently, the cows had thought the grass looked better on the other side of the fence. Cody had to repair the fence before he could leave for church.

Hannah was her bubbly self, following the church service, asking if she could ride to Dave's house with Kara. It was none too soon to catch up on all the activities she had been involved in as of late. Kara was able to share some about her stay with the Madison family. Arriving at the house, the three women got busy in the kitchen, their conversation moving along as fast as their hands. The Ralston men chose to keep Davey company while he put the finishing touches to the cooked chicken by grilling it with barbecue sauce. The location of Davey's home among the trees was quite a contrast to the open range of the Lazy R Ranch. The ranch had fewer trees by far, although there were plenty of trees in the mountains near the ranch.

Hannah and Rita both enjoyed the contrast, exclaiming over this or that as the two took a tour of the place. They had known Davey for nearly two years, yet had never managed to visit him at his home. He had always had an invitation to the ranch, so it had never materialized for them to come here.

Since the air had a fall chill to it, everyone was glad to eat in the kitchen. They shared plenty of good food and laughter. Now and then, Kara cast a sideways glance toward Cody, who was doing the same. It was enough for now to be in the same room as the young widow, so far as he was concerned. Every time Kara laughed, it sent a chill of delight up his spine, and he wished with all his heart he could hear that sound until they were old and gray. He didn't believe he would ever tire of it.

After clean up, they played a game of dominoes. They talked about nothing terribly important. The calves had been weaned and sold for feeders. Cattle prices weren't what they had hoped for, but were tolerable.

After some time, Cody won the game. Time was getting away from the ranchers by then and they regretted having to leave. As the Ralston's stood, Martin said, "Hannah and Cody, why don't the two of you stay a while longer? All of you seem to be enjoying yourselves, and there's nothing pressing at home that I can't take care of. Besides," he said dryly, "it would do my heart good to know that you both had some sort of social life, other than cows and rodeos."

Noting the obvious pleasure on Kara's and Davey's faces, it did not take much to convince Hannah and Cody to stay.

Kara brewed fresh coffee for everyone else and prepared herbal tea for herself. Hannah gave her a hard time. "C'mon, Kara! How do you expect to be a true Montanan unless you learn to appreciate a good cup of strong, black coffee?"

Kara wrinkled her nose and shuddered. She preferred a decaffeinated beverage in her condition.

They decided to watch a video and enjoy some fresh popcorn. Cody offered to crank the handle of the popcorn popper on the stove top. Kara gratefully accepted his help as she gathered the bowls for popcorn and a plate of cookies to munch on. Cody enjoyed her closeness and the perfume she was wearing. The aromas of her perfume and the popcorn were a pleasant combination to his way of thinking.

After the video, they fell into easy conversation, all of them enjoying being able to relax for a day. Talk eventually turned to family and relatives. Hannah wanted to hear more about the wedding Kara had attended, to know all the little details. Conversation changed to the house and belongings. Kara indicated various antique pieces of furniture around the living room. She made it clear to Davey that once the furniture arrived, it would go with her wherever she went, knowing she could not live forever with her brother.

Kara was eager to tell her friends how she had shared her testimony with the Madison family, as well as Tim Werner. She felt confident that good would come from her conversation with the family since they had not shut her out completely, agreeing to give some thought to what she had said.

"Who's Tim Werner? I don't think I've ever heard you mention him," Hannah asked, glancing toward her brother. Cody was suddenly very busy with invisible cookie crumbs he had discovered on his pant leg. Hannah could have kicked him about then. She dearly loved Kara and was somewhat aware of her brother's feelings toward the widow. She couldn't believe he was so slow in making his feelings known to Kara or at least making some kind of endeavor toward a relationship.

"He's a friend of my late husband's," Kara replied with a gleam in her eyes. "Actually, he was a fellow classmate of ours, so we go back a few years. He was with my husband the day he died. Tim has carried so much guilt over Jonny's death. To receive the news from my in-laws that I was with child weighed him down even more. I was able to witness to Tim what the Lord has done for me and how he too could have salvation. Like the Madisons, he promised to give it some thought. He has even purchased a Bible and has been reading it and calling me with his questions. I'm not sure I qualify as the right person to provide the answers but, with God's help, I am confident he is going to be saved."

Clearly, both Kara and Davey thought a lot of this Tim. Neither Hannah nor Cody cared to speculate what it all meant. It seemed a good time to end the visit and get home.

✥ ✥ ✥

En route to the ranch, Cody was quiet, not caring to talk. Hannah was feeling miserable herself, aching for the hurt and disappointment her brother was surely feeling.

"You know, it could be that Tim is nothing more than a friend. Maybe we're jumping to conclusions," Hannah finally said, breaking the silence and desiring to comfort Cody.

"Maybe," was the only comment Cody would offer. At present, he would like nothing better than to crawl into a hole somewhere.

Heaving an exasperated sigh, Hannah blurted, "So, are you just going to roll over and play dead, never telling Kara how you feel about her? I mean—don't you want to give it a try? You're not going to up and quit before you at least share with her from your heart, are you?"

Cody shrugged helplessly, overwhelmed with the seeming turn of events, as he focused his attention out the windshield and on his driving.

Upon entering the house, Cody immediately retired to his bedroom, failing to speak to anyone, which was definitely not his true nature. The Ralstons were a close family and were always willing to share the day's events with one another.

It was a heavy-hearted Hannah who filled in her parents on what had transpired that evening. They agreed with Hannah's suggestion to Cody, but they also stressed that it was Cody's life. As much as they would like to press the issue, the best course of action was to pray for him and to not interfere. He had to figure it out for himself and to turn to the Lord. Martin suggested also that Cody might be drawing some wrong conclusions.

. . . 25

It was now the month of November. With only about six weeks to go in her pregnancy, Kara was beginning to feel as though she would be pregnant forever. Joyce, her midwife, had assured Kara that she was doing fine and the baby appeared to be average size in its development thus far. Things were progressing, and the baby would be born before she knew it. Kara was not so sure. She was beginning to feel like a waddling light bulb. She wished Jonny were with her to comfort her and promise he still loved her, even when she looked and felt this way! Well, the Lord must know what He was doing, or He would have made a different way for babies to be born. It did not help matters when Davey would sometimes tease her about her shape, though as of late he was choosing instead to encourage her.

The normal, everyday chores seemed a hardship now. Once seated in the office chair, she wanted to remain there at times. She had not gained too much weight thus far, but she felt she was getting lazy about taking walks as she should. She just did not have the energy.

Shortly after the harvest potluck and hayride, Kara had begun Lamaze classes with Bobbie and Hannah as coaches. Hannah explained she was not about to miss the birth of this special baby. She had decided Cody would have to figure things out for himself. Kara was like the sister she had never had, and she wasn't about to give up their friendship because of her brother and his feelings. Both Hannah and Bobbie attempted to encourage Kara when she appeared on the verge of tears at times, wishing for Jonny, wishing the baby had been born yesterday, etc. The two hoped that when they were pregnant some day, they had a caring, tender husband to support them. They knew it was difficult for Kara to be alone.

✢ ✢ ✢

Cody himself was struggling with his emotions, only of a different nature. He desperately loved Kara and was not sure how he should go about expressing himself. He noticed how Kara's eyes had shone that Sunday at Davey's house. Was it because of this Tim she talked about? The rancher felt confused and frustrated, uncertain as to what he should do. He begged the Lord for wisdom almost daily concerning the situation, but thus far no answer had come to him. There was a certain consolation knowing the wedding band was still on Kara's finger.

Martin and Rita both sensed the struggle their son was having, yet they felt that unless he approached them about it, they should keep silent and pray.

✢ ✢ ✢

Thanksgiving was only one week away. Rita had been biding her time to see what kind of move her son would make concerning Kara. She wanted to invite Davey, Kara, and Bobbie for the holiday dinner but was uncertain how to go about it. She did not want to make her son miserable being around Kara, but she realized how lonely the holidays could be without immediate family. She was sure Kara would not be up to cooking a turkey with all the trimmings. Deciding on her next move, she waited for the right timing.

The opportunity was not long in coming. Cody entered the kitchen that very day for a cup of coffee to ward off the chill of the biting November air. As of yet, they had not had snowfall, although there was snow on the mountains.

Whispering a prayer to the Lord, Rita appeared normal and nonchalant as her son helped himself to a cup of coffee and took a seat at the kitchen table to enjoy fresh-baked, chocolate chip cookies—his favorite. Rita thanked the Lord for what seemed an open door. Having Cody alone and in good humor, eating his favorite cookie, was an answer to prayer indeed.

It was not unusual for Rita to take the time to sit and chat with her family, but Cody was somewhat wary. He could tell his mother had something on her mind as they made small talk about nothing in particular. After a while, Cody gave his mother a lopsided grin.

"OK, Mom. Out with it."

"What?" Rita asked, feigning innocence. "Well, there is something, only I didn't know how to ask you."

"Ask me what?"

"Next week is Thanksgiving, and I wanted to invite Dave, Kara and Bobbie, but I wasn't sure if I should."

"Well, it's your house. Do as you please," Cody commented, a little too sharply.

"Cody Lee Ralston, don't you talk to me in that tone of voice!"

The young rancher meekly hung his head, staring into his coffee cup. "I'm sorry, Mom. I don't mean to be so ornery."

"Cody, I don't want to make you miserable or uncomfortable with having Kara here. We're aware of how you hurt." Next she was going to do what she and Martin had resolved not to do. "Have you considered approaching Kara about your feelings or at least finding out how she feels about this Tim Werner? It seems it would only be the right thing to do. How's the dear girl supposed to know anything if you don't come out with it?"

"I—don't know, Mom," Cody said with a helpless shrug of his broad shoulders.

"Get bold! If you want Kara bad enough, you'll put forth the effort. You do love her, don't you?"

"Well, yes." This was the first time he had admitted this to anyone. He had spent a lot of time since Sunday trying to convince himself otherwise. Really frustrated now, Cody raked his fingers through his hair, his head bowed down with the weight of his cares. Oh, who was he trying to fool? He did love the woman!

"I love Kara too. A mother wants her children to be happy. All your dad and I want is your happiness. You have our blessing, Cody, whatever you decide, but I'm thinking you'd best not let this woman pass by without a fight. At least think about what I've said, OK? We're praying for you. And since this is my house, as I was reminded, I am going to invite the three for the holiday." So saying, Rita decided she'd best get busy doing some household chores that needed her attention, giving her son a pat on the shoulder as she passed by.

    Cody sat for a time in deep thought, his cup of coffee growing cold. As if coming to a decision, he rose from his chair to plant a kiss on his mother's forehead as he passed through the house to go outdoors.

    For a moment upon entering the kitchen, Rita stared at the chair her son had occupied. Then she looked toward Heaven, sighed, and continued about her business.

... 26

Everyone was glad for a break in their busy weeks as they gathered for Thanksgiving dinner. Kara had made a delicious cranberry Jell-O salad and a pumpkin roll to complement the meal. Bobbie contributed an attractive, tasty yam dish and pecan pie. The rest was left for Hannah and Rita to do. The mother and daughter worked well together in the kitchen. Hannah offered to give her mother a break and suggested she be the one to rise at 5 A.M. to put the big bird in the oven to slow roast. The delicious aroma of the roasting turkey and stuffing drifted through the house, causing everyone to anticipate the coming feast to be held later in the day.

Martin and Cody moaned and complained with humor that it wasn't fair to tempt a person, telling them they will have to wait. With a twinkle in his eye, Cody promised the cooks he would return for a cup of coffee later in the morning to check on progress and to be sure they were doing things right. Hannah punched her brother's arm playfully and told him to tend to his own business outside, namely the cattle.

Rita smiled, hearing her children banter and laugh. There had not been enough of that lately. She prayed that her son had reached a decision concerning Kara. It would be wonderful to see the two make a match of it. Well, she had to stay out of it and leave it be. The Lord was more than capable of handling this.

... All Things Become New ...

The guests arrived at eleven-thirty that morning to help. Since the dining room was reserved for such occasions, Bobbie and Kara set about adding a few finishing touches to the table. Kara had purchased an attractive autumn-design runner for the table, while Bobbie presented the centerpiece she had created just for this day. It consisted of cattails and dried flowers, complemented by fall-colored leaves of brown and gold. Hannah brought out the good china, silverware, linen napkins, and goblets. Then she placed candlesticks on both sides of the centerpiece for the finishing touch. The women stood back to admire their handiwork, as Rita entered to fuss in wonder at the transformation to her table. It made the gathering seem more special, creating thankful hearts at the goodness of the Lord as well.

The three men had been biding their time in the family room, when they were called to the table. They were surprised to see the elegant table laden with food and fancies set before them. They had dressed in decent clothes but felt slightly underdressed for the occasion. Rita shushed their complaints, declaring they did not have to feel unwelcome at all. It did not hurt to have a bit of fanciness, even though she knew the men were more interested in the food itself than in how it was served.

As head of the household, Martin said grace, purposefully praying a blessing for the women present who had done so much to make the meal and day special for them all. As was always the case when they got together, the food and fellowship were wonderful and enjoyable. Kara and Cody glanced in the other's direction now and then, each desiring to know what the other was thinking, especially Kara, who was feeling sensitive about the fact that she was very pregnant. She wished to appear attractive to the young rancher, but she was insecure about her appearance and feelings. Knowing it would do no good to mope on such a special day, Kara busied herself by helping with the clean up after the meal. The men moaned as they sought the sofas in the family room to relax with cups of coffee while their meal settled. Dessert would be served after a while, when they could enjoy it more.

The women worked, laughing and chatting as though they had known each other forever—just like family.

Afterwards, Kara wished to see Rebel, but she noticed the women were too engrossed in conversation about a quilting project

Hannah had begun, so she thought it best to wait. It would soon be dark, and Rebel was in a pasture somewhere on the ranch. Kara was wondering what to do when Cody approached her about that very concern.

"Do you think you're up to visiting your horse?"

"Oh, yes!" Kara exclaimed, her face beaming. "I was wondering what I should do about it when you came along. Perfect timing!"

Cody looked a bit sheepish. "Well, I have to confess it was the thoughtfulness of your brother and not me. He mentioned you had been lamenting over the fact that you hadn't seen Rebel for some time, wishing you could go for a horseback ride. I'll take you to see him, but there's no way you're going to ride."

"You don't have to worry about that," Kara said with a sigh of disappointment. "I don't think I could fit in the saddle right now anyway, and I might break Rebel's back."

Cody, noting the sarcasm in her voice and the fatigue on her face, assured her that she didn't weigh close to what he did and that Rebel supported him fine. Cody knew from his friends who were parents that a woman can be sensitive at times during pregnancy. Kara had mentioned during the meal how active the baby was at night, when she wanted to do nothing but sleep. She did look uncomfortable with the growing baby. She had resorted to wearing her brother's jacket for warmth, which did nothing for her sensitivity.

Cody assisted her down the front steps of the house and to the barn for a special surprise before taking Kara to see the horse, refusing to explain himself. Opening the door to the tack room, Cody led her to an area sectioned off with plywood. Kara knew what he wanted to show her before she saw them. Eight adorable Labrador puppies, eager for attention, scurried to the side where the two stood. The proud mother was none other than Pepper, who looked on as Kara squealed like a small child in sheer delight, kneeling to scoop up as many as she could. It was a picture indelibly marked in Cody's mind for all time and eternity as he watched her, enjoying the beauty of the girl who was the very image of womanhood with her round abdomen. Cody was brought out of his deliberation when Kara spoke up with a wistful expression on her face.

"I've never had a dog of my own."

"Really?" Cody asked, interested in what she had to say. "I suppose living on a ranch, I've taken having a dog for granted. It

. . . All Things Become New . . .

seems we've always had a couple of dogs around the place for as long as I can remember. I think everyone should have a dog sometime in his life."

Kara spotted the only yellow pup in the litter and scooped her into her arms. "I wish she were mine."

Cody smiled knowingly. "Yeah, she's a nice one all right."

Glancing at his watch, he realized with surprise that time was passing. "Say, we'd better get to the pasture if we're going to see your horse."

Kara reluctantly placed the puppy on the straw. She felt embarrassed to have to ask Cody to help her up. Her feet had fallen asleep while kneeling in the straw, and she was having a difficult time of it.

Cody assisted her to her feet. When she felt able, the two walked to the ranch truck. He mentioned that he had ridden Rebel that very morning to check cattle. The gelding was a good one. Cody enjoyed riding the gelding as much as Rebel liked being ridden.

Having brought a small amount of oats in a bucket to attract the horse, Cody drove into a pasture near the ranch house and whistled for Rebel, who was with several other horses. Ears perked forward, the paint and two other horses came to the whistle. Cody haltered Rebel and poured grain on the ground for the other two.

Kara had the privilege of holding the bucket of remaining oats for her horse to enjoy. It was so good to see her horse again. She felt bonded to the animal and longed to be able to mount up and ride into the wind on this crisp, November day.

Cody offered to feed the bucket of oats while Kara brushed and fussed with the horse, talking to him in a soothing tone. Cody could not help but be envious of the horse. Taking a deep cleansing breath, as though he thought oxygen would improve his thinking, Cody was about to launch into a more personal conversation when Kara stepped in an impression in the ground, causing her to turn her ankle. Losing her balance, she fell hard on the ankle with a cry of pain.

Alarmed and feeling helpless as he watched everything happen as if in slow motion, his hands holding the bucket and horse, Cody was beside himself. Putting space between the horse and Kara, he let go of the lead rope and bucket to hurry to Kara's side. Cody helped her stand on her good foot, better enabling him to assist her to the truck. Scooping Kara into his arms, he hurried to the truck to examine the ankle. Cody expertly removed the shoe and sock Kara was wearing for a better look.

Kara was embarrassed that once again she had messed things up in her clumsiness. She could only glare at the offending foot in her anger and frustration. The ankle was already beginning to swell and was sensitive to the touch. It was not sprained, but it was bruised and needed an ice pack. Cody started the truck engine to warm the vehicle before releasing Rebel from the halter and retrieving the now empty bucket, attempting to make Kara as comfortable as he could. Seating himself behind the steering wheel, Cody encouraged Kara to lean against him since her leg with the injured ankle was extended on the seat.

Kara was glad she did not have to look at Cody in her embarrassment. How could she face the others back at the house? Some day this was turning out to be!

✤ ✤ ✤

Kara had a sofa to herself as she settled in for a while with an ice pack on her ankle. It had not been as bad as she had imagined it would be. Of course, Rita fussed as she went about helping Kara get comfortable. The older woman had noticed the baby had dropped into a better position in the last few days. She hoped the slight accident would not promote labor. But Kara was young and strong and would probably be fine, although it certainly wouldn't hurt to keep an eye on her.

Everyone, except Kara, helped to serve dessert, and the day progressed without much more ado. The three men left the house to feed cattle, Davey jokingly offering to boss the job.

Kara catnapped on the sofa as the other women chatted. It was not long before the men were back and ready to eat leftovers for dinner.

Kara wanted to sit at the table with the others. Cody suggested she not put too much weight on her foot. Assisting her in taking a seat, he placed the injured foot on an extra chair with a pillow.

Davey suggested that she stay home the next day and pamper the injured ankle. Kara did not want to be fussed over, but she was out-voted by the others. Defeated, Kara agreed with her brother, placing a call to a woman who sometimes filled in for her or Sandy when the need arose.

Hannah proposed that, considering her condition, she stay at the ranch the next day. Kara did not want to impose, but it seemed she had no say in the matter. The others had decided what was best for her. Kara surrendered, feeling heavy-hearted and defeated, although she wasn't sure why.

✢   ✢   ✢

Once again, Kara was in the capable care of the two Ralston women. If she was honest with herself, she would admit she did enjoy the extra time for woman talk. Cody had expertly wrapped the injured ankle for Kara before allowing her to hobble around the house with the aide of Hannah, who joked about the fact that she had helped Kara in much the same manner not long ago. Kara could see the humor in it and reminded Hannah that the last time she had stayed with them had been the turning point in her life.

Cody was hoping to have time alone with Kara, but it never transpired. Everything that could go wrong did. First, some of the cows broke through a fence, as though some wild animal had spooked them. Then, the main truck the Ralstons used for nearly everything on the ranch broke down and needed major repairs that had to be tended to right away. Martin had gone to an auction, leaving Cody and the hired man responsible. Up to his elbows in grease, Cody could only mutter something under his breath as the hired man helped. Cody's assistant knew something major was bothering the young rancher, who was usually quite congenial but who was very quiet today.

Kara secretly hoped to talk to Cody at lunchtime, but the man seemed preoccupied with something. It was as though he nearly avoided her. Kara was confused and disappointed. She knew she was not the most attractive person in this stage of her life, but that would change given time. Did Cody ever consider having a wife and children? She couldn't think of anyone other than Cody whom she wished to fill the role in her life. However, she did not feel it was her place to approach him and express her feelings. Why did life have to be so complicated? Uncertain as to what she should do,

Kara prayed that the Lord would give her wisdom and show her if this man was for her.

Disappointed that Cody was late coming to the house for dinner that evening, Kara ate and then told Hannah that she would like to go home. Her ankle was tender, causing her to hobble, but she was learning to take things slow and easy.

Alone in her room that night, Kara knew what was in her heart and what she must do. She had thought a lot about Cody that day—the way he looked at her while conversing, the warmth of his steady blue eyes. Could he love her?

Hobbling toward the dresser where her jewelry box sat on top, she opened a small drawer to reverently place her gold wedding band with the other rings. It was time.

. . . 27

KARA'S ANKLE HAD HEALED QUICKLY, MUCH TO HER RELIEF. SHE DID NOT feel she could cope with a bothersome ankle as well as a baby on the way and the longing in her heart that the baby have a father and she a husband. Since making the Lord her life, He had brought about a healing of her heart she hadn't thought possible. She knew she would see Jonny again some day; the peace she had confirmed it. To be alone for the rest of her life with a child to raise was not what she wanted, and she was confident the Lord did not either. Kara was hopeful that should she see Cody again, he would express what was in his heart. Cody was easy to be around, and yet there was an invisible something that made them seem miles apart. Did he have the same thoughts and feelings she had? Kara was not to have an answer as soon as she would have liked.

✤   ✤   ✤

Three weeks to go in the pregnancy, Kara was feeling especially restless one Friday. She had insisted on working up until the baby was born, if she could. Davey and Drew both agreed to it, as long as she was up to it. Sandy thought Kara's stubbornness was to prove some sort of point and told her so. Kara agreed but continued to work. If she was too tired to think, then she would not make herself miserable wishing for some sort of relationship with Cody. Maybe it was all her imagination anyway. Still, her heart told her otherwise. Kara was looking forward to the weekend to catch up on chores around the house and to relax with a good book.

✣ ✣ ✣

Kara had a restless night after she retired that evening. No matter what position she chose, she could not get comfortable. Tossing and turning on the bed, she was up and down, hoping that moving about would help. The thought had crossed her mind to call Joyce, but she hated to impose on the midwife, imagining that with four children of her own, rest was always welcome. Once Davey knocked on her door to be certain she was OK after noticing her bedroom light was on. Assured that everything was fine, he told her to wake him if she needed anything.

Kara counted the minutes and hours on the clock for a while then managed to doze off. At 4 A.M. she was awakened by a mild contraction. Startled, she lay still to see if it had been her imagination. The clock by her bed said twenty minutes had passed before another contraction. This could be it—finally! Elated with the idea of holding the baby in her arms, Kara lay in bed digesting the thought. Suddenly, she sat upright in bed with the realization that the baby was not supposed to be born for three weeks or so. She was hoping for a Christmas baby or, better yet, a New Year's baby. She prayed in her fear that the baby would not be born for another week or two. It just could not be! But it was obvious the baby had other plans, as the contractions continued to come in regular intervals.

Kara waited until 6 A.M. to call Joyce. By then she was nearly in tears to think her baby might be in danger. Joyce assured her that it would have been better had the baby waited another week or two, but it was out of their hands. Every precaution would be taken to ensure the baby would be taken care of after it was born. Kara had the option of going to the hospital if she felt more comfortable, but she chose to calm down and let her body do what it was supposed to. She was certain she wanted the baby born at home. Had it chosen an earlier date, the situation might have been more serious. Joyce had the nursing staff on standby at the local hospital and an ambulance crew alerted, should complications set in.

... All Things Become New ...

Kara called Bobbie next. Bobbie prayed with Kara over the telephone that the Lord would be her peace and would keep the unborn baby safe. Bobbie promised to call Hannah. The floral shop would close at noon. Bobbie and Hannah decided that Hannah would go immediately to Davey's house and Bobbie would join them as soon as she was able.

A sleepy Davey knocked and walked into the bedroom. Seeing Kara out of bed and in her robe, he said in a gravelly voice, "I thought I heard you talking. Were you on the telephone?"

"Yes, I was talking to Bobbie," Kara answered, sounding slightly agitated in her anxiety.

Davey frowned with concern. "Is everything OK?"

Kara heaved a sigh, wishing she could stop the mild contractions she felt every twenty minutes. "I suppose so, but the baby is on the way!"

Davey was instantly awake and pacing the floor in his excitement. "Oh my, is there something I can do?"

"Not really," she assured him. "I'm still in the early stages of labor. I called Joyce too. She is confident the baby might be small but will be healthy. I need to trust the Lord that everything is going to be fine."

Kara asked Davey to read some scripture verses to her until the others arrived. Davey took Jonny's Bible from the nightstand and began reading Psalms. The words soothed Kara's worries like ointment on a wound. Filled with a peace that she and the baby were the Lord's, she was able to relax as the contractions continued.

Hannah arrived, breathless in her excitement. She fussed with the pillow and bedding as she talked to Kara, attempting to soothe the woman and make her as comfortable as she knew how.

Rita offered to come by later to help in any way she could. A new birth was always a time of rejoicing, and this baby would be no exception.

Davey had taken himself to the kitchen to make coffee and stay out of the way. Birthing was something he was not familiar with. He called Drew to explain he wouldn't be finishing the detailing job as he had planned. Drew promised Davey the job would wait and that he and Sandy would be praying that mom and baby would do fine—early or not.

... Audrey Marr ...

It was nearly 10 A.M. when Hannah sought out Davey to inform him that the contractions were fifteen minutes apart and that Kara was being a real trooper.

Joyce arrived about then. She always liked to spend extra time with first-time mothers, to calm and encourage them in any way she could. Upon examining Kara, she was pleased to note the baby was in the proper position.

"It's just a matter of time and patience now," Joyce said.

As the intensity of the contractions increased, Kara patiently bided her time. After a while she chose to slowly walk around her bedroom, sometimes sitting in her favorite chair for short durations. Hannah occasionally rubbed her back, attempting to soothe Kara in her fatigue. It had been a long night and would be an even longer day. Joyce continued to offer moral support and encouragement, as well as prayer. She noticed the peace on Kara's face and whispered thanks to God.

✢ ✢ ✢

"Will you accompany me to Dave's house?" Rita asked Cody. "I thought you could help to occupy his time while the baby is being born."

"I'm not sure I'm qualified to—" Cody began.

But his mother would hear no excuses, barring illness. A reluctant Cody drove his mother to Dave's house.

Davey looked fatigued as Rita and Cody entered the house. Rita assumed kitchen duties, placing a pot of homemade soup she had brought on the stove to warm up. She knew Kara was not up to eating, but the others would be hungry.

Davey was glad for the motherly woman's presence, as well as Cody's. Time was moving slowly; he worried about Kara and the baby.

Cody was a bit distracted, making weak attempts to converse with Dave, all the while straining to hear any sounds coming from the occupied upstairs bedroom.

Rita could see both men's minds weighed heavy with concern over Kara. She decided it was a good time for her to go upstairs and inquire. She returned in a short while.

"You two rest easy. Kara is doing fine. She's looking rather tired but at peace."

. . . All Things Become New . . .

With her words, the men visibly wilted on the couch. Rita grinned at the pair, wondering what they were going to do when the baby being born would be their own!

At about noon, Bobbie entered the house without knocking. "I hope I'm not too late for the main event!"

Davey gave her a lopsided grin as he took her coat. "You haven't missed the birth—I promise."

Bobbie sighed with relief and flew up the stairs to Kara's bedroom.

The men were beginning to wonder if the day would ever end. At one point, Davey said he hoped he did better with his own wife. He was getting a head start on all of that, especially since he wasn't even married. Once, when Cody released a frustrated and tired sigh as he paced the floor, Davey gave him a hard time about the fact that Cody had been waiting only a few hours, while he himself had been awake since 6 A.M. Cody could only shrug his shoulders and give his friend a wry grin, since he couldn't argue the point.

✥   ✥   ✥

Bobbie and Hannah were to either side of Kara as she knelt on a padded sheet. Joyce smiled and reassured Kara, telling her what a good job she was doing. It was not going to be long now. The water had broken fifteen minutes earlier, and the contractions were coming with greater intensity at shorter intervals. Time seemed to stand still as Kara concentrated on each contraction, using the breathing techniques she had learned and practiced in Lamaze class. One of her coaches would rub her back or gently wipe her forehead with a cool cloth while the other encouraged Kara to breathe and relax. As she released a moan now and then, Kara was beginning to appreciate that giving birth was hard work and a lot of it.

Rita kept plying the men with refreshments, which they consumed distractedly. They stood by should she be called upon for any reason.

It was not until 4 P.M. that baby Madison chose to be born. The contractions were so close and Kara so weary, she was beginning to think it would never happen. What a joy and relief to welcome the new baby! Once the baby's mouth was clear of any mucous, Kara was able to hold the wee one while still on her knees, marveling at the miracle she held in her arms. The other women rejoiced and gave thanks to God for the wonder of it all. As soon as the placenta had been expelled and mother and baby cleaned up, the two were made comfortable in bed together. Kara was not willing to part with the baby just yet. The others understood and appreciated her motherly feelings and allowed her some privacy while they had some refreshments.

Joyce walked over to Davey, delighted to be the bearer of good news. "Davey, you are now an uncle. Mother and baby are doing just fine. Baby Madison is a bit small but made of tough stock."

The women looked on in amazement as Davey let out a whoop, taking the stairs two at a time in his hurry to see Kara and the baby. Coming to a skidding halt outside the door, he decided he had best contain himself, or startle the baby.

Tired but elated, Kara lay on the bed with the baby held in the crook of her arm. Davey quietly approached the bed to sit on the edge and study the newborn in wonder. Wetting his lips, he spoke softly to his sister. "Wow! Look at all that jet-black hair. Is it a he, or a she?"

Kara smiled at the reference to "it" before answering, "'It' is a girl."

"Jonny would have been so proud of her, Kar."

This brought tears to Kara's eyes. She could picture Jonny in her mind's eye, acting much like her brother was. Even as young as the baby was, Kara noticed her dimple—like her daddy's—on her left cheek, as well as her blue eyes, although Joyce had reminded Kara that it would be several months before knowing the true color of her daughter's eyes. Kara had always liked Jonny's and Davey's blue eyes, and she secretly hoped the baby's would stay blue.

Kara asked if Davey had phoned the Madisons back east about the baby coming. Davey admitted to having a weak faith. He had been waiting to see how everything turned out before calling and causing them undue concern. He sure hadn't wanted Kara to be rushed to the hospital. One never knew about these situations.

Cody was standing outside the door, hoping to see the new arrival too, when Kara spoke a sudden thought to Davey. "You need to call Tim and let him know about the baby too. The last time we talked, he was getting excited with the idea of her arrival. I'd like to talk to him while you have him on the phone, OK?"

Davey had to go downstairs to get the telephone numbers. In a rush, he failed to notice the paleness of the rancher's face as he met Cody on the way out. Cody had heard every word Kara had said about Tim. He felt sick to his stomach. He knew this was not a good time to be romantic and come out with his true feelings for Kara, especially when the baby wasn't his. But he had hoped for a chance to express himself sometime in the near future. It appeared as though Kara's feelings had not changed for Tim Whoever-he-was.

Consumed with disappointment and defeat, Cody willed himself to ask to see the baby. He was feeling worse as he poked his head in the door to observe the homey picture Kara made holding the baby in her arms, looking weary but content. As Cody approached the bed he wished with all his heart this woman belonged to him.

Keeping the secret thoughts to himself, he could not help but marvel at the sight of the wee one with one tiny, curled fist held against a chubby check.

Kara smiled wearily. "I know she's only an hour old, but what do you think of her?"

"I can see she's going to be a beauty," Cody replied in a hushed voice. *Like her mother,* he thought to himself.

Noticing Kara's fatigue, he excused himself.

Davey arrived, out of breath from running the stairs yet calm as he talked to the Madisons, never explaining the real purpose for the phone call. He gave Kara the cordless telephone, allowing her to be the bearer of good news while he studied the baby some more. Kara had explained that babies are somewhat red at birth but that the coloring would change in a short time. It suddenly dawned on him that he had forgotten to ask the baby's name. He listened intently as Kara announced the birth of Joni Elizabeth, who was five pounds and six ounces. Davey was certain Jon would've liked that name.

Rita soon brought Kara a bowl of soup and crackers. Then Rita left Kara in Hannah's capable care for a week or however long the new mother thought necessary. She overheard some of the conversation with Tim and gathered that he was quite happy for Kara and eager to see the two. She knew it was none of her business, but she wished with all her heart that her son had declared himself to Kara before things had gotten this seemingly serious with Tim What's-

. . . Audrey Marr . . .

his-name. Rita was suddenly weary from considering everything and glad to go home with her son.

Joyce examined Kara and baby one last time before taking leave. Mother and baby were fine as could be.

It was strange but comforting to hear the sound of a crying baby that first night.

. . . 28

<small>L</small>ITTLE JONI THRIVED AND GREW, GAINING WEIGHT DAILY UNDER THE tender loving care of her mother. She was a happy, contented baby.

It was only a few days until Christmas, and Kara was beside herself with excitement. Alice and Jon Madison were coming to see their new granddaughter, and Tim had asked if he could come with them to visit and to see the baby for sentimental reasons. Jonny had meant a great deal to all of them. Kara was excited for Tim to meet all her friends and to perhaps attend Bible study. She secretly hoped his visit would be the time he would come to know the Lord. It was both Kara's and little Joni's first Christmas in Montana.

Kara could not believe how much the baby had already changed in appearance in her few weeks of life. Kara busied herself making suggestions to Davey about how this or that decoration would look nice in the house. Davey humored her some, refusing to allow her to do much around the house, recommending she not overdo.

Jon, Alice, and Tim arrived the day before Christmas. Alice had hoped to arrive sooner, but it seemed everyone wanted to fly during the holidays, so she had to be thankful they were able to get tickets at all. Most anxious to meet their first grandchild, the two grandparents cuddled the little girl with tenderness, struggling with tears that wanted to surface with the realization that she was their late son's daughter. There was no doubt that this was J.J.'s baby. She had the same coloring of both skin and hair as their son's. Kara told them about her daddy's dimple too.

Alice took over the duties in the kitchen. At Kara's suggestion, Davey had purchased a ham for the holiday dinner, as well as all the other necessary ingredients. Kara and Alice had discussed the menu the week before so all would be in readiness.

The Christmas Eve menu included oyster stew, bread sticks, and spinach salad.

Kara was content to relax and allow the others to do the necessary chores. Little Joni was a source of delight for the new mother, who never tired of caring for her, marveling now and then at the goodness of the Lord. Often, while holding the baby and studying the wee girl's features, Kara was fascinated and thrilled with the idea the baby was all hers.

Tim was taken with the baby but uncomfortable with the thought of holding her. Alice promised that he would do fine and that no harm would come to him or the baby, as she placed Joni in his arms. Talk was centered on the baby girl, who was sure to steal many a heart in the days to come. Kara was certain Joni's eyes were going to be blue. It was a comforting thought to have a part of Jonny with her always, if the Lord was willing.

✤ ✤ ✤

Christmas Day was beautiful with the ground blanketed in white snow. The pine trees were covered with snow too, adding to the winter wonderland, creating a Currier & Ives scene.

The first order of the day was to exchange gifts. Little Joni got more things than one child could possibly use, from toys to clothes to more practical items. Kara told the others she would have to be careful or the baby would be spoiled. The other adults only laughed, certain that would not be the case.

Everyone enjoyed the meal. Alice was a wonderful cook. Because of the family business, she seldom had time to show off her culinary skills, but on this special day, her talents shone. There was a festive air among those gathered for the meal. It was almost like a celebration with the baby girl safely among them! Kara suddenly recognized the Lord's timing was right. To have little Joni present for the holiday season was an added pleasure and a salve applied to the wounded hearts of loved ones, as well as her own.

While spending time in her room to nurse the baby privately, Kara reflected on the baby Jesus who came to earth to be born of a virgin that the world might be saved. Being a new mother herself, Kara wondered how Mary must have felt to gaze upon her son and to know how special he was. Kara thanked God for sacrificing His son for her and those she dearly loved, who had as of yet not come to Him. But she was confident that in the Lord's timing, it would come about.

Kissing the top of her daughter's head, Kara thanked the Lord, as she had many times before, for the wee one. The Lord was good indeed.

✣   ✣   ✣

Tim had planned to give Kara time with the baby following the Christmas meal. When he deemed it appropriate to interrupt Kara, he approached her bedroom door to knock lightly. Given permission to enter, he found Kara burping the baby on her shoulder. With a full tummy, the little girl was content to rest where she was placed.

Kara directed Tim to the extra chair Davey had placed in the room for visitors.

Tim acted both excited and nervous about what he wanted to tell Kara. Who better to share with? Clearing his throat, he told Kara his news and how he felt—to the delight of his friend. What a wonderful thing to happen on Christmas Day! The two parted with a great deal of joy and happiness.

The Ralston family arrived for dessert at 4 P.M. Jon and Alice were pleased to see their friends again. They immediately began to share happenings from back home and to boast of their new granddaughter. Rita and Hannah could see for themselves how much the baby had changed in features in only a week.

The Madisons introduced Tim. The Ralstons could see the young man was indeed pleasant and likeable, an obvious longtime friend of the family. The Madisons thought highly of Tim and spoke nothing but good of him, to his embarrassment. Once, Kara placed the baby in Tim's arms, teasing him about making a good daddy someday and saying he might as well get some practice. Tim was practiced enough in holding the baby to realize she would not come to harm after all. He delighted in cuddling and talking to Joni, even though she was too small to fully appreciate the attention.

Cody struggled with his emotions as he watched Kara and Tim obviously enjoy each other's company, as well as the baby. However, there was something amiss. He couldn't figure out at the moment what it was. He sought to follow through with his Christmas plans—regardless. He had placed his gift in Davey's garage.

Davey was aware of Cody's Christmas present and suggested his friend ask Kara to the garage before having dessert and coffee. Cody hesitantly approached Kara with his request. This was not at all the way he had hoped to present the gift. The rancher had fancied himself walking Kara to the garage for privacy to declare his love for her. He imagined she would be elated and would graciously accept his love, stating her love for him in return. The fact that it was not to be was clear to him now. Kara had known Tim Werner for many years—more than she had known Cody. It would seem logical she would fall in love with and marry her late husband's friend.

Kara was puzzled by Cody's request but, after all, it was Christmas, a holiday of surprises. Joni was sleeping soundly in the arms of her grandfather as Kara retrieved her coat. Cody offered to help her with the coat, enjoying the mild scent of Kara's favorite perfume. Had the circumstances been different, he would have been excited about the opportunity to be alone with Kara, but he guessed it was all out of his hands.

Entering the garage, Kara heard the excited whimper of a puppy and understood immediately what Cody was about. Approaching the portable dog carrier, Kara quickly knelt to release the puppy, which was all over her in no time, grateful to be released from the pen. Kara laughed with sheer delight as the pup licked her hand and face, crawling all over her in excitement. It was the one yellow Lab puppy that she had wished for many times since seeing her among Pepper's litter. She had been disappointed when Davey informed her the pup had been spoken for a few days after their visit to the ranch. While caressing the pup, Kara watched as Cody tied a red bandana around the puppy's neck. "She can't be a true western dog unless she wears this," the rancher said with a crooked grin.

Kara looked toward the rancher with a coy smile. "Cody Ralston! That was a mean thing to do to me, causing me a lot of undue stress and sadness believing I could never have this puppy!"

Cody smiled faintly but refrained from looking at the woman he loved. The smile disappeared altogether as he noticed the wedding ring was gone from Kara's finger. He paled with the realization. It was plain to see events had moved right along since Tim's arrival. Cody had to give the man credit for not wasting time where Kara was concerned. What better time for the man to declare himself than Christmas? Come to think of it, Alice Madison had told his mother about the beautiful ring Tim had given Kara shortly after they had arrived, but Cody had not paid much attention. It all made sense now. Maybe she chose not to wear the ring for the time being until an announcement was made to everyone.

Cody's thoughts were interrupted as Kara spoke again. "I'm bursting with excitement and have to tell someone the news about Tim! There hasn't seemed to be time yet when I could tell Davey, and I know you would understand."

Cody did not want to hear about Tim Werner and the life he would have with Kara. Cody supposed they would return to the east to make a new life together—the three of them. The very thought of it made him sick at heart. He had been foolish to put it off as long as he had, having only himself to blame. Feeling how unfair life was with this turn of events, Cody lashed out at Kara in his frustration. "Save your breath, Kara. I can already guess what you have to say, and I'm not in the mood to hear it!"

Kara was shocked by Cody's behavior. It was obvious the man was angry about something, although for the life of her, she didn't know what. "Has Tim said something to offend you, Cody?"

"No, of course not," he answered with sarcasm. "He's been the perfect gentleman and will make a great father for your baby."

Kara was really confused now. She couldn't understand how Cody had arrived at this conclusion! Suddenly, she was angry that the man could be so rude. He should have at least allowed her time to tell him about Tim before making a fool of himself. Kara's green eyes flashed in her anger. Cody was about to receive what he justly deserved. "How dare you be so—so rude and thoughtless! I assumed we were friends to the extent that you could allow me to tell you what I wanted to say before jumping to conclusions. It's clear to me I don't know you as well as I thought I did."

"Conclusions? It's more than obvious what's going on with you and Tim. There's nothing to explain. I hope you're both happy." So saying, Cody arose from where he had been sitting on a box. "Please express my regrets to the others. I think I had better take my leave."

Remaining on her knees with the puppy, Kara was in total disbelief at what had transpired. She had thought the two of them got along well together, that there had been a certain look in Cody's eyes when he spoke to her. Until now, there had only been Jonny in her life, so she was no expert where men were concerned. Shaken, Kara thought she should return to the guests before she started to cry.

Kara entered the house with the puppy only to hear her daughter crying with hunger. Davey suspected there was something bothering his sister when he asked about Cody. As Tim began petting the puppy, Kara gave him the leash with the excuse that she needed to feed the baby. She was glad to retreat to her bedroom, if only for a half-hour. Christmas was supposed to be a special day, a time of happiness, not heartache. The one person she had hoped would notice the change in her—and not just her salvation experience—was gone in his anger. She was not sure what to do.

✤ ✤ ✤

The evening of Christmas Day proved to be a pleasant one, in spite of the dark cloud that prevailed over Kara. The Ralstons were easy people to be with. They had been surprised to hear Cody had left before dessert and coffee were served, but they said nothing, presuming Kara's presence was too painful for their son to stay long. Because they cared deeply for Kara themselves and observing the fact that she was upset about something, they chose to keep conversation light and pleasant.

The Madisons and Tim were leaving in a few days. The Ralstons invited them all to visit the ranch before returning home.

✜ ✜ ✜

Kara was able to share with her brother the next day about what had transpired with Cody. Davey rolled his eyes in exasperation. He was sorry Cody was obviously hurting over the misunderstanding of what was only a friendship.

Davey placed a comforting hand on her shoulder. "Given the chance, I'll speak to Cody about your relationship with Tim."

Kara shook her head adamantly. "No, Davey. This is really between Cody and me. If we fail to communicate our thoughts and feelings to one another now, then we definitely need to learn how to work out these misunderstandings, if we are to have a future."

Davey respected her decision and said he would be praying.

✜ ✜ ✜

Kara, Dave, Tim, and the Madisons went to the Lazy R Ranch for a visit the day before their departure. After so much food over the holiday, the Madisons requested something light for a meal.

Rita made taco soup with breadsticks and salad for her guests. When Cody did not make an appearance by mealtime, Kara asked Hannah where he was, disappointment obvious on her face. Cody had been asked to haul bulls to a ranch hours away. With some other ranch business to attend to, he would not return for a few days. Had her brother been around, Hannah would have taken him aside and given him the tongue-lashing he deserved. No one had questioned Cody about Christmas Day, figuring it was his business. If he wanted to share with them, he would.

Tim, Davey, Hannah, and Kara played a game of dominoes while the other adults visited in the kitchen. Hannah thought that while Tim was not what one would call handsome, he was fun to be with. Kara encouraged Tim to share with the three of them what had happened to bring about his conversion.

Tim's brown eyes lit with pleasure to be able to talk about his experience. "I'd been running from the Lord for a long time, to be honest with all of you. After Jonny accepted the Lord, I was under severe conviction. It wasn't until Kara came for the wedding and talked to me about the love of God and shared her testimony that I realized my need for Him in my emptiness and guilt. But I no longer feel the guilt connected with Jonny's death, since receiving Christ. I'm attending church and reading my Bible. I guess you could say I'm finally finding fulfillment in my life."

Davey patted his friend on the back. "Just be sure to keep on reading the Bible. Be patient with your Christian walk, and keep your eyes on the Lord, Tim."

Tim smiled in appreciation.

Joni never lacked for arms to hold her as she was passed around throughout the evening. The Madisons did not care to stay late with the early flight in the morning. Tim, the Madisons, and the Ralstons said goodbye and promised to keep in touch.

... 29

KARA SETTLED BACK INTO A ROUTINE AFTER THE VISITORS RETURNED home. She was anxious to return to work, but Davey would hear none of it. He thought there were enough household chores to keep her occupied, from what he could see. Joyce had stated that six weeks was early enough to return to work, and that was the way it was going to be.

Davey and Kara—and Joni, of course—had been invited to spend New Year's Eve with the Ralstons. Kara was somewhat responsible for how it had all come about, and she wondered if she had taken advantage of their friendship. But she was beginning to feel nearly desperate in desiring to speak to Cody. Her anger had dissolved a long time ago—on Christmas Day in fact. She knew how she felt and decided that all that was needed was the right timing. Thinking back on the last conversation she had had with Cody, she remembered seeing the pain reflected in those dark, blue eyes of his. She had never meant to hurt him in any way, and never in her wildest dreams had she suspected that he was in love with her. Not once had he suggested he cared for her as more than a friend.

Kara's chance came when she boldly approached Rita after the church service following Christmas, asking if her friend had made any plans for New Year's Eve or New Year's Day. Rita could not believe that Kara would be up to cooking for a crowd. Rita insisted that she, the baby, and Dave come to the ranch for the celebration to welcome in the new year.

"Why not bring extra belongings and spend part of the next day with us?" Rita added. She was weary of seeing her son mope around the house, and she hoped the relationship between Cody and Kara would be patched up, whatever the disagreement was about.

❖   ❖   ❖

New Year's Eve day entered with four inches of fresh snow carpeting the ground. Kara loved to look out the windows of Davey's house to admire the panoramic view before her. The pine trees were blanketed with fresh snow; the air was crisp and clear. The azure blue sky was cloudless, contrasting with the green and white of the trees.

Leaving the house with the baby in her arms, Kara breathed deeply of the air, taking pleasure in the beauty of the day. Just last night she had determined in her heart that one way or another she was going to speak to Cody privately and explain some things, even if she had to tie and gag the man with the help of her brother. He was going to listen!

❖   ❖   ❖

Kara had made up her mind to enjoy the evening with the Ralstons and to bide her time. Cody was cordial but quiet during the meal. Shortly afterward, he excused himself to tend to a few animals in the barn.

Cody was surprised Kara was still in Montana and surmised she had duties to attend to before making plans to leave for the east. He was somewhat puzzled to note there was not a ring from Tim on her left hand. While at the table that evening, Kara had showed the diamond and ruby ring Tim had given her for Christmas on her right hand. Cody's brow furrowed as he considered this new revelation. Could it be he had made a complete fool of himself on Christmas Day? He had regretted his behavior many times since then. He had rudely cut her off and failed to allow her to speak.

Not too long ago his own mother had been angered by his rude bluntness.

Plopping on a bale of straw, the rancher studied on the situation awhile, glad for the privacy and quiet of the barn. He loved the different smells of a barn—the hay, the manure—odors that only a rancher could love. It was going to take a little time to sort out what he should do. What to do? That was the question . . .

✤   ✤   ✤

Kara became increasingly restless as the evening progressed and Cody did not return from the barn. Impatient, Kara passed Joni to Hannah and went to the kitchen. Rita was putting together a tray of munchies and brewing a fresh pot of coffee.

"Rita, how long does it usually take Cody to do chores?"

The older woman had noted through wise eyes that Kara had been unsettled all evening. Little Joni had been fussy too, and she was not generally a fretful baby. Attempting to act casual, she remarked, "Oh, he could come in most any time."

"But three hours, Rita? I don't know much about feeding animals, but I'm certain that with only a few animals in the barn, it can't take that long." Kara sounded exasperated.

That's a good sign, Rita thought. *I always felt she had brains and spunk!* She concealed the smile creeping across her lips and busied herself with the tray of food. Kara was too beside herself to notice.

Unexpectedly, Kara asked, "Rita, can we talk? I have some questions that need answers."

"Sure, dear. I've got all the time in the world. What is it you want to know?"

Each of the women took a chair in the kitchen to get comfortable for a lengthy discussion. Kara was determined to get answers from someone, and Rita seemed the most logical choice.

✤   ✤   ✤

It was ten o'clock at night. After some soul-searching, Cody was seeing himself in a truer light, and he did not like what he was seeing. He dreaded having to go inside and face Kara. He could not

... Audrey Marr ...

believe what he had done to the poor woman. Of all the people he had not wanted to hurt, she was at the top of the list.

About the time he had decided to humble himself and face the music, taking whatever Kara dished out to him, he heard the barn door open and close quietly. He suspected it was his dad checking on him. As the person stepped out of the shadows, Cody was surprised to see Kara instead. She looked beautiful as ever with the glow from the pale light in the barn illuminating her. She smiled. Never in his wildest dreams had he expected that smile. He was speechless as Kara stepped closer.

Holding up her left hand, she said, "I removed it for you."

"What?" Cody questioned, failing to grasp her meaning.

"The ring," she replied with a slight flutter of her left fingers. Tears pooled in her green eyes. "I did it for you, Cody—not Tim."

"But—but—I thought Tim and you were making plans of some kind Christmas Day."

Nodding her head in disbelief, thinking that it was just as Rita had explained, she said, "YOU, sir, never gave me a chance to tell you what it was I had wanted to say. Remember? You cut me off by wishing me well, etc., etc."

Cody looked at the toes of his boots in his shame. She was right and he knew it.

Kara sat beside Cody on the bale of straw. "Cody, please understand. I didn't come out here to argue with you. I came out here to explain how I feel and to clear up any misunderstandings. First of all, the ring belonged to my grandmother and then my mother. It was showing years of wear, and I wanted it reset by a jeweler. While I was back east in September, I came across it in my belongings. Tim offered to take care of it because he had an out-of-town friend who was a reputable jeweler. Presenting the ring at Christmas was a surprise of sorts by Tim. He was aware of my sentimental fondness for the heirloom.

"Secondly, what I wanted to tell you about a week ago is that Tim has accepted the Lord. He has been attending church in our hometown and going to a weekly Bible study. He says it's the best thing that has ever happened to him, and he regrets not having done something about it sooner. He grew up in a Christian home but went his own way when he became an adult, much like you said you did. He also met a woman in church whom he hadn't seen since high school. She had been away at college and had decided about the beginning of December to move back to her hometown. They're seeing one another on a regular basis. Isn't that neat?" Kara's eyes sparkled with enthusiasm, stirring in Cody a love he had thought was dead with all the hurt he had been feeling. But it was there, as strong as ever.

Cody looked into Kara's eyes, his voice husky with emotion. "Kara Madison, I love you!"

Kara placed her hand on the side of his face and spoke softly. "You have no idea how I have longed to hear those words these past few weeks."

Cody wrapped her in his arms, pulling her close to him. The scents of her clean hair and her perfume nearly made him lightheaded. He was intoxicated. That was the word for it: intoxicated! Love was a beautiful thing indeed! The two sat holding on to each other, cuddling and enjoying the solitude, hearing only the sound of horses munching on their hay.

After a while, Cody glanced at his watch. He and Kara turned to each other, smiled, and said simultaneously, "Happy New Year!"

The barn echoed with laughter.